At once elegant and funny as hell, Bob Butz has written the most useful book I've seen all year. Everyone will be needing this book. No exceptions. See you at sunset.—*Doug Peacock, author of* Grizzly Years: In Search of the American Wilderness

PRAISE FOR GOING OUT GREEN

Think of *Going Out Green* as a responsible owner's manual for death. Until I encountered this book, I imagined my family packing my remains into the hills on a mule, sticking me in the ground whenever they got tired of walking. Thanks to Bob Butz, I see that I should do a little more planning if I want to leave this world with the same level of care that I've used to live in it. This book is a must for anyone who might someday die—and yes, I'm talking about you.—*Steven Rinella, author of* The Scavenger's Guide to Haute Cuisine *and* American Buffalo: In Search of a Lost Icon

Plain and simple, *Going Out Green* is a fun book to read. No kidding. From start to finish, Butz's sharp wit and matter-of-fact way of addressing the topics of life and death. He neither waxes poetic nor comes off preachy—he merely invites readers to come along for the ride of discovery. And if more people would talk about death and dying in the demystifying way that Butz does, I, for one, believe we'd be much better off as a society.—*Wendy Lyons, president, Funeral Consumers Information Society*

A light-hearted introduction to a heavy subject that's going to be of increasing importance to Americans. The book raises important questions for anyone contemplating eco-friendly end-of-life rituals.—*Joe Sehee, Executive Director, Green Burial Council*

D0168260

He not busy being born is busy dying. Bob Dylan sure got that one right. Restated: If we and our loved ones are temporarily vertical right now, we and they will be permanently horizontal before we know it. Consequently, it's never too early to start paying attention to the terrifying fact (or reassuring blessing, depending on our worldview) that personal death is not only inevitable, but in the big picture and long view it's essential. While death and its attendant ceremonies should be, and in most cultures for most of humanity's history were, viewed as a dignified culmination and celebration of life, our overly urbanized, perhaps terminally "civilized" contemporary humanity has largely forgotten it. We have turned it all over to a macabre and financially vampirish, chemical-smelling funeral industry; a darkly spooky dirge orchestrated by sallow strangers in it for the bucks. In *Going Out Green*, through his own journey of research and learning, author Bob Butz provides us with the information and inspiration we need to recapture control over our own deaths, thereby enriching our lives. A wonderful, uplifting little book whose relentless sense of humor is utterly appropriate. —*David Petersen, author of* On the Wild Edge: In Search of a Natural Life

Going Out **GREEN**

Going Out **GREEN**

One Man's Adventure
Planning His Own Burial

BOB BUTZ

Cover design by Barbara Hodge

Cataloging-in-Publication data for this book is available upon request. ISBN: 978-0-9818708-1-6

First Printing 2009

10 9 8 7 6 5 4 3 2 1

Contents

For my father

The First Week

Wherein the adventure of planning a green burial begins.

I have three months to plan my own burial.
The sentence is easy to write, but try saying it out loud at a cocktail party. Even if you happen to be a writer with a history of pursuing weird stories, people will think that this time you can't possibly be serious.

"You're doing what?" a friend said to me last night. "What the hell for? Are you dying or something?"

Near as I can tell—and even though it's admittedly early in my research—being buried almost always involves first being dead. And death, like politics, is a real downer of a conversation topic even if you do have something interesting to say.

Realistically speaking, I know we're all dying. But as far as I know, right now I am not terminally ill; though, come to think of it, in high school I was once in an algebra class labeled "terminally stupid" by the teacher who also believed the condition as incurable as it was communicable. Teenagers he considered infected—namely all of us—were labeled "a bunch of jerks" and were apparently so beyond help we weren't worth talking to, let alone teaching. So for 45 minutes every day, when he wasn't staring out the second-story window as if he were seriously contemplating the leap, poor Mr. Schaffer would just sit in the chair behind his desk doing nothing, shoulders sagging in a defeated slump. He didn't so much look at us as look through us with the same gaze of helpless bewilderment I catch on the faces of those who hazard to ask me what exciting new project I'm working on now.

Planning what to do with your body after you're done with it is supposed to be a dour activity of the old and infirm. People die all the time (again, my preliminary research is showing this is true) and, depending on the source, statistics say 57 percent of dead people go with a conventional burial.

About 25 percent now choose cremation. The Cremation Association of North America has long projected that figure to increase to 36 percent by 2010. And now, for the rest, there's an increasingly popular option called a natural or "green" burial.

The Green Burial Council loosely defines a green burial as one that rejects "formaldehyde-based embalming, metal caskets, and concrete burial vaults." Simple, personal, inexpensive, environmentally responsible . . . and, it must be said, nothing new.

Muslim and Jewish religions have always maintained eco-friendly funeral practices. In fact, not so long ago every burial in America was what they're now calling green. When Aunt Clara keeled over cranking up a pail of water from the well, no funeral director was called to cart the body away. The family made all the arrangements: washing, dressing and caring for the body as it reposed in the parlor; building a plain, pine-board coffin and digging a grave under the apple tree on the ridge overlooking the Back Forty.

Today, most people pay strangers to do all the dirty work. According to a recent news release from the National Funeral Directors Association, the average funeral costs in the neighborhood of $7,500, a price that "does not take into account cemetery, monument or marker costs, or miscellaneous cash-advance items, such as flowers and obituaries."

Conventional burials are costly, arguably unnatural and not exactly great for the environment. According to statistics compiled by Mary Woodsen, a Cornell University science writer and VP of the Pre-Posthumous Society of Ithaca, New York, America's 22,500 cemeteries annually bury approximately:

827,060 gallons of embalming fluid, which includes formaldehyde

180,544 million pounds of copper and bronze in caskets

30 million board feet of hardwoods, including exotic woods, in caskets

3 billion, 272 million pounds of reinforced concrete vaults

28 million pounds of steel in vaults

For people like me whose minds start to drift when people spout numbers with this many zeros, Joe Sehee, of the New Mexico-based Green Burial Council, put it this way in a recent article for the *Detroit Free Press*:

The annual casket consumption in America winds up burying enough metal in the ground to build and rebuild the Golden Gate Bridge every year, enough embalming fluid to fill an Olympic-sized swimming pool, and enough concrete to build a two-lane road from New York to Detroit.

And what about all the toxic herbicides used to keep the grass of conventional cemeteries perfectly manicured, totally weedless and golf course green? What about all the land in this country set aside for conventional cemeteries, land that is pretty near worthless for anything else once you start stockpiling dead people there?

I'll admit I'm a land-lover. Although a reviewer once called me a nature writer, I've never been accused of being an environmentalist. I do what I can where the planet is concerned, but thanks to a mortgage payment, two needy kids and a wife with a bizarre affectation for buying truckloads of what I contend are absolutely identical black shoes—"life" in a word—I felt obliged to turn in my Birkenstocks about the same time I could no longer stuff everything I owned into the back of my silver Honda Civic. At this point, I doubt very seriously that "going out green" will come anywhere close to rectifying the environmental mayhem I've wrought simply by virtue of my being born, not to mention my trying to enjoy life on this planet for the last few decades.

Green burials came to interest me because, frankly, all the traditional ones I've seen over the years were a real drag. They left me thinking that there had to be a better way.

The first funeral I attended was my father's, when I was eleven. Over the course of nine months a brain tumor turned my once strapping dad into a skeleton with sore, ashy skin. He died at home. The ambulance came and took him away. The funeral director, I'm sure, did the best he could. But three days later, lying in his polished, frilly oak casket, my dad was so pumped full of fluid he looked ready to pop. He had makeup powder on his face, rosy lips and cheeks like a doll.

My dad never wore a suit. If he did have a closet fixation with doing himself up in women's cosmetics, I certainly never heard about it. Dad wore a buckskin vest every day of his life, with faded denim, boots and big brass belt buckles depicting snarling bears and leaping whitetail deer. He was a man who used to do pushups with me on his back. He once killed a deer on top of the mountain behind our house and carried it the whole way home across his shoulders so as not to ruin the hide, which he later tanned and had turned into a pair of saddle-colored work gloves.

When you're the son of a man who dies young—my father died at only 35—you tend to think about death and how it all might play out a lot more than other boys your age. Growing up with that memory of my father as a dead man so bloated, waxy and unrecognizably outfitted made me pretty much decide that when I died, I wanted it to be in a mysterious or heroically incendiary manner that left nothing behind but a scorch mark. I wanted to leave bare elegant bones to later be discovered and marveled at (nod to the writer Edward Abbey)—or nothing but a good story or two and a memory of what I was the day I walked off into the woods to never be seen again.

Looking back on it now, I guess I imagined myself "going out green" before there ever was a term for it.

So one day last September when Heather Shaw, my friend and soon-to-be-editor, called and asked, more or less, "Hey, how would you like to write a book about planning your own burial?" the idea of it didn't strike me as a stretch . . . until she told me the deadline was only three months away and that the publisher had very little money to float for an advance. After that, the conversation went a little something like this:

"Three months?" I said, incredulous. "That's some deadline. Har. Har. But seriously, what do I know about planning a green burial? I'm no expert."

"That's why it's so perfect. I'll send out the contract."

"Twelve weeks," I said. "And the money? Do I really have to die in the process of writing it, too? I have a family, you know. Bills to pay."

"Just sign it and drop it back in the mail," she said.

"You're not hearing me," I said.

"This is going to be great!"

Heather is the kind of woman who commonly starts sentences with phrases like, "So I was sitting there on the top of a mountain in the Andes thinking . . ." or "When I was living in Mexico married to that guy in the CIA . . . ." I have known her for years. She's a smart and beautiful lady friend, who like all smart and beautiful women, tends to be unaccustomed to men resisting her advances.

"Look at it as a challenge," she said. "Most people your age who die don't have any money at all and less than three days to plan something. Plus, if you did kick off between now and then, imagine what the story would do for sales."

A couple days later I found myself surfing the Internet, digging up facts (so to speak) on the green burial movement in America, boning up (just one more, I promise) on green burial preserves, and uncovering the supposed dirt (there it is) on conventional burials.

Where bio-degradable coffins were concerned I spent many hours trying to decide if my character was more suited to being buried in a six-sided Boot Hill-style pine box or a sleek and ultra-modern Ecopod made from 100-percent recycled newspaper with softly silk-screened images of flying birds on the outside. I found coffins made of compressed cardboard, woven wicker and scraps of reclaimed lumber. Yes, I spent a considerable amount of time perusing coffins looking for one that defined me as a person.

I made arrangements to tour a natural burial preserve and wondered what it was like to hand-dig a grave. My office filled with books about death-midwifery, an art still practiced by a small but growing collective whose expertise in caring for human corpses allows regular people to confidently take charge after the passing of a loved one and manage a dignified funeral and burial service at home.

It all sounded so right and so simple. In fact, one of the appealing and reoccurring themes of a green burial is that it should be a simple affair. And part of the purpose of this slim volume was to find out if that was true. I wanted to find out for myself—a person who admittedly knew absolutely nothing about burial of any kind—if in three months it was possible to figure out all that was required to plan a so-called natural burial.

In this book, I talk a lot about what I found, but I haven't created a reference guide. Neither is this a history of the natural burial movement in America. I can't even promise any profound insights into what it's like to contemplate one's own burial. This book is simply an effort to chronicle and honestly report my efforts to understand what exactly is required when planning to return naturally to the earth.

The Second Week

 Wherein a memory of worms offers a glimpse into the future.

One summer, when I was small, I had worms. Cul-de-sac dwelling suburbanites might assume I'm talking about one of those worm hobby kits you can still occasionally find alongside Uncle Milton Ant Farms (*See the ants . . . Building Bridges . . . Digging Subways . . . Moving Mountains!*) on the dusty, bottom shelves of small town toy stores. But my worms taught me absolutely nothing about natural underground ecosystems and the wonders of organic composting. Thirty-odd years gone by and I still struggle to find the most dignified way of putting this. Of course, when I was five, it literally came out so easily: "Mommy, come quick! There's a worm coming out of my butt!"

Dirt is, well, dirty. When your playground is a farm, there's a lot of it around. Intestinal parasites, like roundworm, are part of the landscape. Sources estimate as many as 55 million American children are infected with some sort of parasite during childhood. Hook and pinworm are two other biggies. But roundworm is actually more common. One University of Maryland Medical Center report I found claimed as many as a billion cases of roundworm worldwide.

Roundworm eggs are expelled in the feces of animals and can live up to seven years in the warm soil commonly found around chicken coops, cattle pastures and pig sties. Not just a hazard for hick country farm kids and barefoot Third World village people with crusty cow plop mashed between their toes, roundworm eggs are also commonly found in suburban sandboxes. The females are big, arrestingly so, if my mother's face as she busted into the bathroom was any indication. The lively nematode dangling from my pale and precious behind made a night crawler look like a puny garden wiggler. Female roundworms—which can grow up to 16 inches long, are as big around as a #2 Ticonderoga pencil and weigh as much— can lay something like 27 *bazillion* eggs in their life. Whether in a barnyard or a sandbox, eggs mix in with the very same soil that is more than occasionally ingested by children who like to stick their fingers in their mouths.

Roundworms are a hard thing to detect because most of the early warning signs—flatulence, nervousness, irritability, poor or ravenous appetite, anal itching and nose picking—also happen to be common symptoms of being a kid. But if left alone, the immature roundworm larvae can travel into the lungs, brain, eyes and liver where they can cause wickedly unpleasant health issues, like respiratory infection, organ damage, even blindness. Usually detection is early enough to prevent these effects, but it can be a shocking experience, as in my case. One minute, the child is literally sitting there on the hopper minding his own business and the next—Hello!—the horrid creature is poking its devilish head out from its hidey hole, so to speak. If, like me, the boy happens to love fishing, there is a relatively good chance that he will be positively tickled (in more ways than one) that his ass has suddenly been transformed into a handy bait dispenser. My mother, on the other hand, had a more predictable reaction: she flipped the hell out.

Mom still gets a shiver whenever she recalls chasing me around, little plastic sandwich bags on her hands, trying to gather an unbroken specimen for the doctor. In typical kid fashion, I couldn't quite see what all the fuss was about. In fact, I clearly remember streaking around the living room not wanting to give the thing up. Alas, Mom ran me down, pinned me with a foot to the back, seized the worm and after gingerly working it free for a minute, gave one last, hearty, two-handed heave-ho, as one might pull the cord on a sticky starting lawn mower.

The University of Maryland Medical Center might insist roundworms are the most common thing in the world, but my pediatrician at the time had never seen one. I'll call him Dr. Lorre because he reminded me of the bug-eyed and sinister caricature of Peter Lorre—the quintessential mad scientist in the Bugs Bunny cartoons I used to love. From the top of his greasy comb-over to the bony tips of his pale, Nosferatu hands, Dr. Lorre embodied all that was creepy. He had old man breath and, worst of all, seemed to take a frightening sort of glee in poking me with his gargantuan syringes. When he wasn't trying to fake me out—"Hey little buddy, is that a spider on the ceiling?"—while ramming needles the size of a telephone poles into my spindly legs, Dr. Lorre would prod my nether regions and various orifices in a manner reminiscent of a veterinarian examining an unruly dog.

"So what seems to be the trouble?" he deadpanned.

As I climbed upon the metal examining table my mother pulled the Glad bag from her purse and brandished it like a bad report card.

One look at the thing and the doctor's head snapped back. In a rare display of emotion, he nodded approvingly.

"Whoa! What a beauty! Where'd you get it, son?"

"It came out of him!" my mother said, leveling an accusatory finger at me. After giving her and then me a puzzled gaze, the doctor composed himself with a heavy sigh and scribbled something on a chart.

"It came out of him where?"

"On-the-toilet."

I recognized my mother's tone: deliberate and threatening. If I'd felt anything for the doctor, I might have warned him to be very, very careful. Don't let the girlish figure, the funky 70's-era permanent and the good skin fool you: my mother could gut a chicken, slop a hog, skin a rabbit, wrestle a calf, run a vacuum with one hand, lift a couch up with the other and still split your britches with a wooden spoon from across the room if she thought you were sassing her. She was a suburban kid before she married my father and went country, which is to say she wasn't a dimwitted rube. She was a woman capable of incredible compassion, patience and kindness, but you didn't ever toy with her.

"It came out of the toilet? Ma'am, I don't understand."

At this place in the story my mother likes to interject that Dr. Lorre had always been an objectionable, condescending little moron. She also likes to point out that he retired shortly after this incident, as if his inability to identify common intestinal parasites may have been the deciding factor in his finally getting out of the pediatric profession.

"It came out of his behind!"

Lorre let slip a dismayed, if not downright irritated snicker. He snapped through the pages in my chart some more, then, after a measured pause, spoke. "Come. Come, now," he said, or words to that effect. "It looks to me like a regular worm. Boys will be boys, you know. Always finding things and sticking them where they don't belong."

Clearly, he was referring to the clot of raisins I'd packed

up my nose a few months earlier. That incident resulted in my being strapped down to a board on the examining table. The extraction itself involved large steel implements more commonly associated with a Civil War surgeon's amputation kit. I blocked out exactly what happened after the first rancid fruit clicked in the steel pan, but I do remember not wanting so much as to look at a raisin again for many, many years.

"Look at it again," my mother said. "That is not a night crawler."

"Ah, I think it is."

"Is not."

And so on.

I can't recall how long this exchange continued. But somewhere between my mother calling him incompetent and him calling in a colleague to possibly restrain her, he made a couple quick calls and consulted a book before finally agreeing that—Holy shit!—heavy doses of prescription medication and a follow-up visit were definitely in order.

With this falls the curtain on my first formative boyhood memory. But given the burial planning project at hand, naturally it got me to thinking: with worms I began, and one day, to worms I would rather like to return.

The Third Week

Wherein the color of death is revealed, meat is made, bones are scattered and vultures carry the spirit to heaven.

Old Arctic Inuit hunters could supposedly sit for days with harpoon poised and ready to strike, staring at a hole in an otherwise desolate sheet of windswept ice, waiting for a seal to surface and steal a breath of air. Enduring frosty cold and, presumably, mind-numbing boredom, the hungry hunter, clad in his mukluks and furry caribou coat, would peer endlessly at his ice hole and enter a hypnotic yet alert state of blissful and cleansing awareness.

All of this bliss aside, death was probably never far from the primitive hunter's mind and, courtesy of my reading material for the last three days, neither was it from mine. After what amounted to 36 hours waiting for an antelope to come drink at the waterhole where I lay ostensibly hidden in ambush with a old wooden bow and a couple of arrows, it occurred to me that the only thing more mind-bending than staring at an ice hole in the middle of a frozen plain was spending three days in a dusty, pollen-choked hay-bale blind reading about human decomposition while periodically staring at an empty puddle of muddy water somewhere in western South Dakota.

Seventy-eight pages into *The Principles and Practices of Embalming,* I learned that green is the first color of being dead. Within one to three days after we have breathed our last, the process of putrefaction for the unembalmed human body begins. Here are some highlights from the text:

One to three days: "Greenish discoloration of the abdominal wall. Odor of putrefaction is noticeable. The eyeballs become soft."

Three to five days: Green patches begin to appear on the genitals, back of the neck, chest, and lower extremities. "A bloody, frothy purge may pour from the mouth."

Eight to ten days: "The green discoloration is general over the entire body." The belly of the deceased begins to bloat and distend.

Fourteen to twenty days: The corpse, including its extremities, becomes blistered and swollen. Hair and nails are "loose and easily detached."

One to six months: Accumulated gases cause the body cavity to "burst." Cranial bones reach a point of decay that allows the brain to escape. Any identifiable features of the body are lost.

A real page-turner, I know. In truth, *The Principles and Practices of Embalming* is about as cheery as a grocery list. It's a classic textbook for mortuary students. Mine is a vintage, second-edition copy from 1959. Make it this far in the book and you discover that a cadaver immersed in water will float anywhere from six to ten days. A corpse with skin showing "dusky red patches" suggests a person frozen to death. You also learn that prior to the Civil War, most of Christian America saw the ancient practice of embalming a human body as a sacrilege or, as Mark Harris described it in his book *Grave Matters*, "a kind of desecration of the human temple of God that was condemned in the New Testament." This attitude quickly changed when the remains of thousands of dead Union soldiers began arriving at Northern train stations, packed and putrefying in sweltering summer railcars. Embalming the dead has more or less been standard practice in America ever since, unless you happen to be Muslim or an Orthodox Jew. The paragraphs preceding "Chronological Order of Putrefaction" also settled once and for all the old dinner-time arguments about what decomposes faster: the dead body of a baby or an adult; a fat person or a skinny one. All things being equal—temperature, rate of exposure to the elements, and so on—if you guessed the former in both instances, you win.

You don't have to be a hunter to understand why waterhole hunting is very near pointless when the whole prairie is lush and green. For months before my arrival in western South Dakota, the state had seen record rainfall, or so I heard. Water, water everywhere meant lots and lots to drink. Not only that, the North American pronghorn is a species built to survive in hot and dusty conditions. Give an antelope a single blade of dewy grass and it'll stay happily hydrated for days. Needless to say, my expectations were low.

Originally, I'd hoped to observe an embalming this week, but that was proving more difficult than I had expected.

"Why would you want to do that if you're planning a green burial?" a friend of mine asked.

I had to think about it for a second.

"I don't know. Maybe to see what I'm going to be missing?"

It seemed I was going to miss it anyway. Two funeral homes back in Michigan never returned my call and a secretary at Wayne State University's department of Mortuary Science in Detroit, after asking me a series of questions I felt were designed to determine if I was a deviant whack-a-do, informed me that with fall classes just starting, it might be some time before someone got back to me. I decided to go hunting.

Pus, snot, mucus, gristle and putrefaction are a few of those super-nasty words that make you wonder where the hell they came from. Webster defines putrefaction as the "anaerobic splitting of proteins by bacteria and fungi with the formation of foul-smelling incompletely oxidized products." It derives from the Latin, of course. But, I mean, really. Some words are just inexplicably abhorrent and they don't always have to have something to do with raging infection, decay and bodily fluids. Take the word "moist," for instance: there is not a single instance or connotation of that word that would ever inspire me to use it in conversation. "Panties" is another one I find so unfathomably icky it gives me the shivers. I even wince writing it down. But I digress. When it comes to words that describe vile human juices and advanced stages of rot, the interesting thing to me is how I've never had a problem with things like pus and putrefaction as long as I don't have to say the words.

Sitting in my little hay-bale fort from dawn to dusk, when I wasn't reading I was watching the birds. South Dakota has a dazzling variety of bird species—over 400! There are towhees, sparrows, juncos and longspurs. Grebes, ibises, falcons, kites, eagles, hawks and sandpipers. Goatsuckers and cuckoos. Plovers out the ying-yang. Waterfowl and warblers out the wazoo. I watched gadwall ducks and Northern Shovelers and the lovely sunny-breasted meadowlarks. A rail and five prairie chickens visited me to water every morning between eight and nine.

For the record, the prairie chicken doesn't look like a chicken at all. About as big as an eastern Ruffed Grouse, it has marvelous cream and brown-colored stripes as if a celestial confectioner drizzled it with white and dark chocolate. They looked so meaty and delicious I might have tried to arrow one if I'd had a license allowing me to do so.

Some people don't believe that hunters really love wilderness and wildlife. How can anyone claim to love something passionately only to kill the source of that inspiration? I've asked myself this question more than once in my life and my first reaction is always one of knee-jerk offense. To hint that hunting is simply about killing is to me as ignorant and wrongheaded as believing a person is somehow closer to God simply by going through the motions of taking a piece of bread and sip of wine every Sunday. For me, hunting feeds my body and soul. It's both a means and a metaphor for living. The immersion is total when playing my blood role as predator. I literally shake sometimes when I think about it—the sweating and bleeding and belly-crawling over a million miles of thorny tangles like a pilgrim climbing to a place of enlightenment at the top summit Mount Kailash. Those who love wilderness and wildlife with every corpuscle of their savage being will understand when I say how—when a hunt is done right, the kill coming as a sacred codifying end—it's like getting as close as mortally possible to touching a sort of Eden.

John James Audubon. Theodore Roosevelt. Ernest Thompson Seton. Aldo Leopold. Edward Abbey. Throughout history, when talking about the best known, most outspoken advocates and protectors of wilderness and wildlife, it's a plain fact that the greatest were hunters.

But I'm not here to change anyone's mind about hunting. Hunting is simply the best way I know to connect with the natural rhythms of the earth, life and death and everything of real consequence in between.

For example, I used to live on a farm where almost all the animals we raised eventually ended up on the table. I don't expect that people who prefer their meat wrapped in cellophane would ever understand how anyone could essentially eat their pets, but there it is. Animals were born. They lived for a while. Then they died. Death might come in an instant with a bullet in the brainpan at butchering time, or it might come painfully, mysteriously, over the course of many months as it did with my father who started falling down, forgetting where he put things and generally acting more than a little bizarre.

I'm not comparing the death of my father to that of a chicken losing its head to make us a stew, but I am saying that this life of living close to the bone—close to the land where people weren't afraid to get a little blood, pus and shit on their hands—helped give me a stomach for the hard and honest realities of living. Seeing death close up made me humble and deeply appreciative of the gift of life. It also made me realize that where the end of life is concerned, many times the animals had it a lot easier, maybe even better, than we did.

Before I spotted the antelope, the only thing moving on or over the prairie was a Swainson's hawk. From my hay bale I could see all the way to the piney hills of eastern Montana and Custer National Forest, a good ten miles away. I watched the hawk soar and periodically flap low over the golden plain until I lost sight of him in the mirage between here and there.

There was no telling how long the buck had been lying there. I looked up from my book and there he was—a small one, facing the other way. I saw the curve of his ears and the tops of his little ebony-colored horns where a moment before there'd been nothing but sage bushes and golden grass in the bright, afternoon sun. I took note of the wind and studied him for a few minutes before deciding to quit sitting around and try to make some luck happen. It took another hour of careful crawling—inching over rocks and prickly pear thorns—to get within a stone's throw.

With a wooden bow and arrows my range is not that much greater than what a mountain lion needs to rush its prey and pounce. I was so close, I should have been able to catch his scent on the wind. I know I tried. I nocked an arrow on the string, gathered my legs under me and tried to calm my drumming heart long enough to shoot. Suddenly, the buck leaped to his feet, and when he did the arrow was gone. One minute the animal was alive and untouchable; the next, he was tumbling dead in a pile of bones, blood, organs, fur and muscle.

Right before I'd focused on the crease behind the animal's front shoulder, drew, anchored and saw the arrow away, I'd caught a lovely glint of light in the buck's obsidian eye. It was what poet D.H. Lawrence called the "quickness."

The quick is God-flame, in everything. And the dead is dead.

Strange to think of poetry when butchering, but this is what I do.

The bones of the antelope I didn't keep to later render into stock, I collected and returned to the sight of the kill. Burying the unused parts of a wild animal I've killed has never occurred to me. Tossing them in the garbage has always struck me as a dishonor, if not a downright sin.

I carried the antelope's remains back to the open prairie—set a femur over here, a scapula over there—and was careful to move the guts around until the scene looked exactly like what a pack of coyotes might leave behind for the buzzards. I always thought this little ritual was my own private creation. Then I read about an ancient funerary practice in Tibet called a "sky burial" in which the corpse of the deceased is placed on a mountaintop to be devoured by vultures. The vultures supposedly carry the spirit to heaven. Even the bones of the deceased are smashed and broken into little bite-sized bits. In the end, nothing is left but a bloody smear on the rocks.

What does all this have to do with putrefaction?
Like death, I suppose, one day rot will happen to the best of us. The only difference is that a body left to decompose in a coffin eventually turns into fetid, putrefied slop. No coffin, no matter how expensive, can preserve a body indefinitely. Industry terms like "protected," "gasketed" and "sealed" are often used to make the purchaser believe that adding these extras will keep a body preserved for a longer period of time. They won't.

An internet article I copied to read on the plane home—sort of a buyer-beware piece from U.S. Funerals Online, a national funeral home and reference directory—made the point most succinctly: "All that these extra additions will do is drive up the price of the casket . . . [but do] nothing to prove your love and respect for the deceased."

What a coffin does do, however, is prevent the deceased from giving anything good of themselves back to the planet that sustains us—all of us—even those who die with praying hands they believe are wholly clean of dirt and blood.

The Fourth Week

 **Wherein the spirit of
a natural burial is
compromised by people
looking to make a buck.**

Only three weeks into this project and I'm beginning to wonder if I'm cut out for thinking about being buried all the time. For one thing, and I know this is going to come as a shock, it's depressing. On the plane ride home from South Dakota, I sat in a window seat with my head resting against the cool, oval glass. Next to me, a tiny Asian woman with a runny nose spent the entire flight from Sioux City to Minneapolis trying to cough up a slug. For two, maybe three hours I stared down from the clouds, watching the world go by, listening to her labored hacking, trying not to cast disparaging thoughts. The rolling prairie turned into a parceled patchwork of green woodlots and golden fields. I saw scattered silos and little houses gradually give way to the civilized geometry of parking lots, subdivisions, cities, towns and the black highways crawling with lines of ant-like cars. The farther east we flew the more crowded and shitty it all looked, until finally, we headed north to the big woods of my home in northern Michigan. I decided I needed a more uplifting topic to ponder—something fun—like maybe deciding on a coffin.

Of all the decisions to make when planning a natural burial, picking an earth-friendly coffin is one I thought would be a cinch. I had in mind a six-sided, wooden "toe-pincher" made popular in old western gunslinger movies. No varnish. No glue. Maybe dovetail joints or dowels instead of nails to hold the thing together. Going online and punching "natural burial coffin" into the search block turned up the website for the Natural Burial Company of Portland, Oregon—"the foremost distributor of biodegradable coffins in North America"—which also claims to have the widest selection of natural burial coffins "at the time."

At www.naturalburialcompany.com you can see eco-friendly basket-style coffins woven with seagrass, banana leaves, willow cane and "Fair Trade Certified" bamboo. There are simple pine coffins made from "wood secured from sustainable managed forests" and another coffin called the "Everybody Coffin" made from molded "formaldehyde-free, multi-layer Ceiba Pentandra wood." There are coffins to suit every taste, every budget. There's a humble and inexpensive heavy-duty cardboard coffin box that stores flat until needed, assembles in seconds and, for only around $100, is suitable for natural burial or cremation. There's also something called the Ecopod.

The Ecopod is a totally biodegradable coffin made in the United Kingdom from 100-percent recycled paper and covered in "handmade paper of mulberry leaves and recycled silk." The Ecopod comes with a choice of exterior color and silk-screen design (Blue-Doves, Red-Aztec Sun, and Green-Celtic Cross) so you can pick what you believe defines you as a person.

To be fair, The Natural Burial Company doesn't actually have a hand in the manufacture of the Ecopod; the company only imports the thing 5,000 miles across the Atlantic for carbon-conscious [sic] people who want to be buried in one. According to the website, so far that's amounted to less than a dozen out of the roughly two million people who die in America every year.

Modeled after a seedpod, the Ecopod was the most un-coffin-like coffin I had ever seen. The Ecopod's inventor, Hazel Salina, came up with the design twelve years ago after deciding the shape of a traditional coffin was too much associated with "negative icons such as Vampires." In my case, her design worked. I can honestly say visions of ghastly bloodsuckers never once crossed my mind when I saw a picture of the Ecopod. Instead, I couldn't decide if it more resembled a whitewater kayak or an escape capsule jettisoned from an alien space ship.

"It looks stupid," my wife said when I called her off the elliptical machine to have a look. Nancy has never been one to mince words.

Another friend concurred with my alien escape-pod observation. Specifically, I was told it looked like something Mork from Ork might have used if the writers of the 80's era sitcom didn't have Robin Williams landing on Earth inside a giant egg.

I had to do some more digging to find a price for the Ecopod (The Natural Burial Company advertises itself only as a wholesaler) and, a couple clicks later, nearly choked on my Morning Thunder.

Shazbot!

Suggested retail price at this writing was $3,400, more than the price of many conventional caskets.

I'm all for capitalism and making a buck, but the Ecopod seemed to run contrary to the fundamental tenets of the natural burial movement. It certainly made no sense from an environmental perspective. In the words of Jim Nicolow, a nationally recognized expert on sustainable design and an environmental professional for American Public Radio's

"Public Insight Network," "shipping a $3,000 recycled coffin 5,000+ miles to reduce a burial's environmental impact feels a bit like selecting the rapidly-renewable bamboo trim package to reduce the environmental impact of your Hummer."

Nicolow's automobile analogy got me to thinking: What is a coffin really but another one of life's boxes we use to carry our dead weight from one place to another? My old silver Honda Civic would be an exhaust-sucking clunker by today's standard, but it's the automotive equivalent of a simple pine box. It always got me where I was going and—at over 50 miles to the gallon—consumed considerably less fossil fuel than any hipster hybrid being made now, 20-odd years later.

"Green burial is not about what you buy, it's about what you don't buy," said Josh Slocum, executive director of the Funeral Consumers Alliance, in a March 2008 edition of NPR's "Marketplace" profiling the Ecopod. "It's about simplicity and economy as much as it is about being environmentally friendly."

You go, Josh.

Moving on, I found American Indian-style, rough wood caskets made of alder with a Pendleton blanket lining, buckskin buttons and a plush Pendleton pillow for $1,995. At Eco Coffins Ltd., another company from the United Kingdom, where green or "woodland" burials have been gaining in popularity since the concept was rediscovered there in 1993, you could select a stock coffin with your choice of exterior mural or motif (e.g. ivy, poppy field, autumn leaves, or imitation wood grain) or create your own design.

On the one hand, I could not fault anyone who wished to be delivered into the hereafter in something that looks like the "wood" paneling on the walls of a mobile home; beauty is in the eye of the beholder, right? Or do I want to say there's no accounting for taste? People have been buried in caskets made to resemble Budweiser cans, giant guitars and space-age torpedoes reminiscent of the capsule in which Kirk placed a dead Captain Spock after the battle with Khan.

I might not exactly get it, but that certainly doesn't make it wrong. The only thing I will say is that all those pricey burial options were enough to make the rebel in me seriously consider what I thought would be the cheapest and least showy option—the burial shroud.

Still a part of traditional Jewish and Muslim funerals, burial shrouds were also used in the Byzantine era by frugal Christian paupers so that a perfectly good set of clothes wouldn't be lost to the surviving family. Sure enough, on one website I found hand-painted shrouds made of raw silk, velvet and something called "African mud cloth" for anywhere from $300 to $500. But seeing such prices for what amounts to a glorified bed sheet made me feel even grumpier. I tried to imagine the type of person who would buy one and kept picturing a condescending Toyota Prius-driving weenie looking to halo their inner Jesus in style.

Of course, the same thing could be said of me. What was I trying to prove by going out in a pine box? That I was a tightwad? That I was a six-shooter-packing rebel? Does it matter?

Well, as long as I'm footing the bill, it matters, and 500 dollars for a shroud was twice the cost of the cheapest wooden box advertised on the internet—what I decided must certainly be the simplest, most unpretentious and cheapest damn wood coffin in America. The recycled items offered by "No Name Lumber," a Minnesota company, offered the aesthetic charm of a shipping crate, a fact the manufacturer made clear:

Our caskets are NOT WORKS OF ART.

I loved the honesty. And I definitely loved the idea of cobbling together something useful out of salvaged material someone else had cast aside as waste. No varnishes. No glue. The wood came from scraps—pieces of pallets, crating, packing and shipping supports.

In the end, however, I wondered if a basic coffin was something even someone with my mediocre woodworking skills should be able to build himself. A handmade coffin from locally harvested wood—I'm thinking traditional pine—not only satisfies the basic green burial requirements of simplicity and economy, it also adds the sort of thoughtful individuality you definitely can't find in a store.

With this in mind I found plans for coffins that convert into entertainment centers, coffee tables and hope chests. I found plans for a peaked Amish-style coffin and a spooky six-sided model that looked like a stage prop from the movie *Salem's Lot.* Yes, it made me think of vampires, but unlike the Ecopod, it wouldn't suck me dry.

Not only did the rough-cut rectangular box with simple rope handles look easy enough to construct, but it also might work nicely in my office as a bookshelf until such time as I needed to use it. On Halloween, it could serve double duty as a most excellently spooky front porch prop. Casket Furniture had plans for such a coffin and, for around $40, promised easy step-by-step instruction.

I placed an order and finished the week confident that my intentions held true to the fundamental green burial principles of simplicity, economy and responsibility to the earth. As much as some might want their coffin to make a statement about their lives, the time for defining who you are is now, while we're actually living life.

The Fifth Week

**Wherein the real lesson
of Edward Abbey's
burial is learned.**

In 1989, George H.W. Bush became the 41st president of the United States. The Soviet Union was busy pulling the last of its troops out of Afghanistan, ending a 20-year failed effort to occupy the country and leaving an entire generation of mountain-dwelling Muslims looking around for another godless superpower to play jihad with. Nine passengers and crew onboard United Airlines Flight 811 were sucked into oblivion 22,000 feet over sunny Honolulu when "a sudden loss in cabin pressure"—a phrase that took on a grave new implication—caused the top of the Boeing 747 they were riding in to spontaneously peel off the plane. And on a hot March afternoon in Pima County, Arizona, at the end of a washed-out and rutted road somewhere in the Cabeza Prieta Desert, four men gently lowered a blue sleeping bag containing the body of their friend, the writer Edward Abbey, into a hastily dug and unlawful grave.

I remember exactly when I first heard about the strange circumstances surrounding the burial of Ed Abbey. Looking back on it now, and given my distaste for the way my father died and was buried, it's no wonder it made an impression on me. Stories like this always stuck with me: the guy who so loved bird hunting that he had his cremains mixed with gun powder and put into shotgun shells which were later handed out to friends; the angler who liked fishing so much he had his ashes ground into bait; and the Sibley, Iowa bow maker, Otis "Toad" Smith, who had some of his cremains put into the handle of a wooden bow. Smith was a catfish angler, too, and such a wild man that after a surgery in which doctors removed a portion of his damaged heart, he soaked the piece in Fish Formula "Catfish Scent," took it to a nearby river, put it on a hook and caught a fish.

Doctors said my father's brain tumor was a fluke, but that didn't stop me from constantly thinking I was only one throbbing headache away from an early grave. Death scared the shit out of me. But for some reason it didn't seem nearly as bad when I read about somebody having their ashes blasted out of a cannon. Or their corpse set ablaze, like the singer Gram Parsons, whose drunken posse of friends in 1973 tried to carry out the singer's last request by stealing his body at the airport, driving it out to his beloved Joshua Tree National Monument, dousing the casket with gasoline and then tossing in a lighted match.

After my father died, the house and farm sold at auction. My mother, brother and I went from being surrounded by wide-open country to a tiny apartment in the suburbs of Harrisburg, Pennsylvania, hemmed in by parked cars and concrete. A swampy patch of woods with a creek running through it became my refuge.

When I wasn't actually hiding out in the woods, I spent most of my angry and alienated adolescence reading books about escaping there: Aldo Leopold's *A Sand County Almanac*; John Haines' *The Stars, The Snow, The Fire*; Henry Beston's *The Outermost House;* Annie Dillard's *Pilgrim at Tinker Creek*; and, of course, *Walden* by Henry David Thoreau.

Thoreau went to the woods because he wanted to "live deliberately." I just wanted to be left alone to track deer and foxes, to watch the birds, to wade in the creek looking for frogs and, basically, to learn my ash from an elm.

Children who lose a parent young learn awful quick that there's no such thing as forever. Toward the end I remember asking my father if he was going to die. He could barely speak at that point, but swallowing hard, he managed to utter a hoarse and unconvincing "no." It sounds so silly now–what other answer could a father have given to his eleven-year-old son?–but for years I held that against him. If you couldn't trust a word from your own father, who the hell could you trust?

My mother worked two jobs. My father's side of the family, after he died, made a lot of weekend promises about coming to visit and taking my brother and me to do things. Aunts. Uncles. Cousins. Eventually, they all fell away. People, I learned, were so unreliable it didn't make a whole lot of sense getting attached to them.

But in the woods you only had to worry about yourself. Nature became my constant. The deer, the red fox, the hawk and the crow became my surrogate friends. Wherever you went, the animals were there if you knew how to find them. The sun rose in the east and set in the west. The seasons reliably changed and the birds always migrated north and south. While other boys my age were reading comic books and Hardy Boys mysteries, I collected Roger Tory Peterson field guides. I read the kind of books that taught you how to build a fire with sticks, fashion a noose from a piece of twine, catch a fish, build a shelter and know which berries, roots and mushrooms were safe to eat. Out in the woods, I always knew where I stood and where I was going. And when I read the words of Thoreau and Leopold, I more than felt that these dead men were the only ones who understood me. Their words were wise, almost fatherly affirmation that what I was doing out there was uncommonly real.

How I came by Abbey's *Desert Solitaire* I have no idea. A couple months away from graduating from high school in 1989, I already had every intention of heading out West to launch my own literary career as a woods-wandering, elk-eating, poetry-penning hermit. *Desert Solitaire*—Abbey's tale of working as a backcountry ranger in the canyons of southeastern Utah—picked up for me where *Walden* left off.

The man who novelist Larry McMurtry dubbed "the Thoreau of the American West" walked a jagged and contradictory middle ground between writer and activist. Abbey was an environmentalist who threw beer cans out the windows of moving cars, a leftist who thought Mexicans should stay on their side of the Rio Grande. At the time I didn't know anything about Abbey's boyhood in Home, Pennsylvania, or his hatred of cattle ranchers, land developers or mineral speculators. I knew nothing of the FBI record suggesting anarchist leanings and ties to radical eco-terrorist groups. I still haven't been able to make it more than a couple chapters through the novel that made him infamous, *The Monkey Wrench Gang*—the supposed inspiration behind the 1980 founding of the radical environmental group Earth First!

But I didn't care about all that. The guy turned what most people overlook into enduring poetry. Abbey made a part of his life immortal with that book, and as a young man, that impressed the hell out of me.

Before Abbey died at his home in Fort Llatikcuf, near Tucson, on March 14, 1989, the 62-year-old Abbey left written instructions about what he wanted done for him. These were recounted in *Adventures With Ed*, by Jack Loeffler, and *Walking It Off*, by Doug Peacock, books written in later years by two of the four men who carried out Abbey's last request:

. . . body to be transported in bed of pickup truck . . . No undertakers wanted. No embalming (for godsake!); no coffin. Just a plain pine box hammered together by a friend; or an old sleeping bag or tarp will do . . . I want my body to help fertilize the growth of cactus, or cliffrose, or sagebrush, or tree, etc . . .

"The very last time—it was just before dawn—Ed Abbey smiled was when I told him where he was going to be buried," wrote Peacock. With a forged death certificate, whiskey and five cases of beer, the four friends sped off into the federally protected Cabeza Prieta Desert, a favorite place of Abbey's, to illegally bury their friend.

"We drove through washes lined with mesquite and desert willow," recounted Peacock, "over creosote-studded bajadas, past cholla and ironwood, driving west with Ed packed in dry ice in the bed of the truck."

It took the rest of that first day and well into the next before they finally settled on a gravesite and dug a waist-deep hole. "[We] slid Ed's enshrouded carcass out of the shade, into the light of the sun," recounted Loeffler. "We loaded him onto our shovel handles and started the last stage of Ed's funeral procession."

Peacock and Loeffler both remember lying in the hole and checking it for fit. Then, working quickly, they lowered in the body. Peacock threw a black vulture feather and letter he had written to his friend into the hole before the men shoveled in a ton of desert soil topped off with a pile of rocks.

"We poured beer on his grave in a final toast," wrote Loeffler. "Then we left our friend to become one with the desert."

I remember thinking when I first read this story that Edward Abbey lived and died in a way most men can only wish for. Abbey proved in death that he was an original. Certainly for me, the story breathed a new truth into my reading of *Desert Solitaire*. I mean, here was a writer who you might not agree with all the time but one who died and was buried in such a way that, if nothing else, you could trust his words came from an honest and unapologetic place. At the time, the strange story was an affirmation that one could take control of death. Abbey's death has, in fact, become legend, which to me not only made the idea of wandering the lonely metaphorical desert of life seem not so bad, it made embracing the solitary, "implacable indifference" of nature seem like a beautiful, enlightening and uncommon virtue.

I could go on regurgitating back-cover bullshit about his gritty plainspoken style or his "naturalist's eye for detail." But at eighteen, to be honest, a lot of what Abbey talked about in *Desert Solitaire* went zooming well over my head. It was his burial that impressed me, for probably the same reasons it impresses many green burial proponents today who regard him as the "first modern green burial practitioner."

What took me 20 years to figure out though, now that I'm sitting here in a comfortable office with photos on my desk of my wife and two wonderful kids my miserable soul would literally be lost without, is that maybe Abbey wasn't quite the loner I always thought him to be. There are, after all, dozens of ways to return naturally to the earth. I can ask to be shot into space, buried in the backyard in a simple pine box, pecked clean by crows or cremated in an energy-efficient incinerator. But in the end it takes more than a carefully dictated note of directives to make it all happen. It takes the will of the living—the hearts of a devoted family and the hands of loyal friends.

The Sixth Week

**Wherein plans are again
altered and the meaning
of a green burial preserve
is explored.**

At ten o'clock on a Friday night, the only thing moving in the headlights on the road outside Bellevue, Ohio, was an Amish buggy pulled by a steaming horse. I tapped the brake and hung back, slowing the Subaru to a crawl, as the horse, huffing spooky clouds of vapor, strained to reach the crest of the hill. When the straightaway came and I saw a safe opening to pass, I stamped the gas and went around, giving the buggy a wide berth. Shifting from second to third, I saw the houses and brick buildings and the lights of town coming up. But I never saw the police car.

I glanced in the rearview just in time for him bounce out of the shadows across the double yellow and onto the road behind me, lights spinning on the roof and the high beams alternately blinking. I said to myself, "What the shit?" or something like it. The needle on the speedometer wasn't even reading thirty-five.

When I found a place to pull over, the squad car eased in tight behind, aiming every white light at the back of my head with the sort of hot and searing intensity commonly associated with alien spaceships right before you're beamed onboard for an anal probe. I felt pretty certain that a conversational equivalent was about to occur given my Michigan plates and the digging tools that lay in plain sight in the back of the wagon and—did I forget to mention?—the .45 pistol tucked under a map in my travel bag on the passenger floor?

We sat there, nobody moving. With an eye on the driver's side mirror I powered down the window and returned both hands to the steering wheel, deciding it best not to try and reach for anything until asked.

The cold October air smelled of horse manure. The stoplight ahead of me turned from red to green. I heard a metal jangle and a clip-clip-clopping and the Amish buggy rattled past. I tried to catch a glimpse of the driver snapping the reins, but a sudden tap on the passenger window jerked my head right where another bright light hit me full in the face—a flashlight so eye-crossingly bright I saw popping white stars as I fumbled for that side's window control.

"Evening," said a voice, manly but chipper, from beyond the blinding glow. "Do you have any weapons or drugs in the car that I should know about?"

"As a matter of fact . . . " I said.

I told him about the pistol and my permit to carry it. Not that I make it a habit of running afoul of the law but, in case you're wondering, the police officers I've met in my travels have yet to be taken aback by a citizen packing a little heat. This one coolly panned the light into the back of the car, settling the beam on the pick, shovels and double-bitted ax.

"Where is it?" he asked.

"Right in my bag," I said, nodding to the pack on the passenger floor.

"Okay. I'll need your permit, driver's license and proof of insurance. You know why I stopped you?"

"Actually," I said, digging in my wallet and handing the stuff over, "I haven't a clue."

"You got a headlight out."

"No kidding," I said. "I just had that thing fixed."

By now my retinas had stopped spinning, so while he walked off to check if there wasn't a warrant out on me, I looked at the map, using the headlights of the squad car.

"Where you headed?" the officer asked a couple of minutes later, stooping to peer into the window.

He was fit and polished, a well-creased and clean-cut looking fellow. Thirty-something with dark, neatly sculpted helmet-hair.

"To Wilmot," I said.

He made a face.

"That's a ways yet."

For a second, I thought I might actually get out of this without any more questions. But then he glanced again in the back at the tools: "What's in Wilmot?"

And there it was.

"A cemetery," I sighed. "I'm going to look at a burial preserve and, if I'm lucky—I mean, if things work out—I'm going to try digging a grave."

He pondered this a second.

"Not yours, I hope."

"No. It's nothing like that. I'm a writer. It's for a book. I'm working on a book about planning your own green burial—"

He cut me off, handing my license and everything else through the window.

"Uh-huh. You're right, that does sound pretty strange," he said. "I'm giving you a warning for the headlight. If you get stopped again—and at this hour, you probably will along this road—just show them this. Good luck."

And then he walked away.

What is a natural burial preserve? Is a natural burial even legal? What about wild animals digging up the grave? What's to stop some crazy from stealing the gold teeth out of a body when it's not even buried six feet under?

These are a few of the questions Jennifer Quinn is routinely asked in her line of work. But my calling out of the proverbial blue and asking if I could come to Ohio, tour Foxfield Burial Preserve and maybe try my hand at digging a grave was definitely a first. I told her about my deadline, explaining that I didn't have much time.

"Do you think you might bury anybody, say, in the next few weeks?" I tried not to sound too hopeful. But it probably came out that way.

"Well, that's a little hard to say," Quinn replied.

In my life I've buried some beloved dogs and a couple of family cats. I once even buried a pet lizard in the backyard after the petrified specimen, spinning defiant circles in the toilet, refused to go down.

At this point, I knew I wanted a handmade pine box coffin. I'd also decided that I wanted my grave to be dug by hand. So, partly in the interests of this story, but more because I've always had this thing about never asking someone to do something I wouldn't be willing to do myself, I wanted to experience what it was like to dig a grave for someone for real.

Quinn made no promises. Foxfield Preserve had opened only that summer, 2008. Seventeen plots had sold on the property since August, she explained, and only three green funerals—one per month—had been held there so far.

"That actually sounds pretty good," I said, mentally calculating the odds. Then hearing the eagerness in the words, I winced. "I mean that sounds like a lot. Very sad."

"Yes it is," Quinn said. Every grave at Foxfield was either hand-dug by the local Amish, or if time was short, by a Wilmot-area excavating crew using a small track-hoe which could tightly maneuver throughout the property without damaging any of the native trees, flowers and grasses.

"Well, I'd at least like to see the place. How about this Saturday? And if somebody dies in the meantime, could you give me a shout?" I asked.

Looking back on it now, I can't believe she didn't hang up on me.

Right off the bat, the biggest problem I found with "green burial cemeteries" is that there aren't enough of them. The first and best known in America—South Carolina's Ramsey Creek—only opened a decade ago, in 1998. I checked out the website for the Natural Burial Cooperative and found that only 15 similar preserves have opened since then in the entire United States. One group in the Midwest—the Trust for Natural Legacies, Inc.—was working on the long-term goal of establishing a green cemetery in every state in the region. I also learned that there's a growing trend among operators of conventional cemeteries—those who see green burial as akin to the birth of the cremation movement 30-odd years ago—to set aside or add on acres for clients who request a green option.

But what are you supposed to do right now if, like me, you don't live anywhere near a cemetery that currently allows vault-less, un-embalmed, un-casketed cadavers to be buried on their grounds?

One state away in Ohio, Foxfield Preserve was the closest natural burial cemetery to my northern Michigan home.

So what's wrong with that? I've read about people having their bodies flown or driven halfway across the country to be buried at a place like Ramsey Creek. Why was I so bothered by a mere 450-mile trek to southeastern Ohio?

For one thing, if you're the eco-minded sort, doesn't it seem more than a tad silly to go to the trouble of forgoing embalming fluid, a casket and everything else if you have to hire a mortuary transport service to cart your remains for hundreds of gas-guzzling, carbon-belching miles to the nearest green cemetery?

I couldn't quite put my finger on it, but my reservations went deeper than the fear of enlarging what must be my already Bozo-sized carbon footprint. The whole time driving south, I kept trying to think of one thing I knew about Ohio. I've really only seen the state at blurringly high speeds while ripping along I-80 on the way to visit family back in Pennsylvania. I like to make this leg of the drive with a full tank of gas in the dead of night when, preferably, the kids are sound asleep in the back. The Ohio turnpike is a grimy, concrete corridor of fast food joints, suicidal semi trucks and disheveled, cranky, strikingly unhealthy, rumpled and road-weary people. I've never had any desire to slow down when going through Ohio, let alone spend eternity there.

But I tried to keep an open mind. My home right now is northern Michigan. My wife and children are here. I guess being buried one state over wasn't totally out of the question. After looking up driving directions to Foxfield, I did a quick Internet search to see what sort of "Ohio tourist attractions" my family could visit if, just for the sake of argument, I took up residence in a hole outside Wilmot.

I expected some mention of the hidden natural beauty

that was certainly in Ohio, somewhere. Maybe a hint of a wilderness park, a mention of a forest—anything.

Topping the list, instead, was Mansfield's "Bible Walk and Living Bible Museum"—*It's like walking through a wax Bible!* My six-year-old son would undoubtedly love the two-headed calf in Brookville, one of the "Fabled Freaks of the National Road." Billed as an insider secret, the Carriage House Museum in Dover supposedly had a wax replica of the Confederate raider William Clarke Quantrill, scourge of occupying Union forces during the Civil War. Stored out of sight "in a vintage refrigerator, alongside a bottle of ketchup and other condiments," his head is something you have to ask to see, presumably with a nudge of the elbow and a wink of the eye.

I had another odd question for Quinn when we met at her office that sunny Saturday morning in October:

"What's a nice girl like you doing in a job like this?"

Quinn was young, hardly 30, soft-spoken, girlish and slender. Dressed in jeans, her hair pulled back, she was the kind of strikingly outdoorsy woman that in another life I would have expected to encounter on a Rocky Mountain hiking trail, or maybe hanging out in the parking lot at a Grateful Dead show. Her hands in her pockets, Quinn told me about being in charge of a cemetery: arranging grave-digging crews, attending every funeral and acting as liaison and burial process coordinator for the family of the deceased. She helped lower every coffin into the ground and, when it came time, helped close every grave.

So how did a gal with a degree in forestry end up here? The short answer: Quinn had had a really bad year.

It started with the death of her grandfather. A couple months later, her grandmother died, then a great-uncle, her great-aunt and, finally, a good family friend.

"Every time the phone rang, it seemed like somebody close to me had died. After attending all those funerals," Quinn remembered, "I decided I didn't want any of that for myself or my parents. Death care today is so removed from the family. There's absolutely no family involvement, which seemed bizarre and unnatural to me."

During that terrible year, Quinn got hooked on the HBO series *Six Feet Under*. She read everything she could about the "woodland" or green burial movement in the United Kingdom and learned that the trend was increasingly catching on here in the United States.

"I was actually considering starting my own preserve in Pennsylvania for a while," said Quinn. "Then a friend told me about the job opening here."

After a lengthy interview, Quinn won out over 30 other candidates from across the country for the strange position that combined cemetery sales and marketing with natural resources management.

Nine years in the planning, Foxfield is the nation's first green burial preserve operated by a non-profit land trust organization, The Wilderness Center. In a media kit, The Wilderness Center was succinctly described as "a self-supporting non-profit nature center established in 1964 . . . to connect people with nature . . . through educational programs, hands-on outdoor based experiences . . . workshops, courses, eco-tours, and walks in all seasons" at its 600-acre facility located in the hardwood hills and Amish farm country of southeastern Stark County.

After a short conversation in the parking lot of The Wilderness Center—a clean brick-and-mortar complex with offices, exhibition halls and even a gift shop selling field guides and butterfly nets—I climbed into the passenger's seat of Quinn's little blue Toyota. The actual cemetery was situated on the edge of the Center's main property, less than two miles away, down a gravel road lined with tangled oaks, maple and locust trees.

We ground past an Amish farm. We slowed for a splotchy brown and white barn cat darting across the road to a white farmhouse and a great red barn. Two men in straw hats, black pants and suspenders were working on rusty and dangerous-looking farm equipment. A hand-painted sign in the yard advertised eggs and pies for sale. I wondered out loud what kind of business the farmer's wife pulled in along this dusty road.

"That's the Mose Miller farm," remarked Quinn, waving through the driver's side window at the men, who acted as if they couldn't see us. I expected a short story about Mose, but Quinn said nothing.

Leaving out the part about my run-in with the law the night before, I told Quinn about driving to meet her that morning and passing through an Ohio I never knew existed. There were tiny country towns with pleasant names like Apple Creek, Walnut Creek, Charm and Mount Hope. I passed through rolling hills with nothing but farm fields as far as I could see; past pumpkin stands selling Indian corn and wooden Amish carts, handmade, no doubt, by good, strong people with German names like Coblentz, Yoder and Schlablat. Here in Stark County, the Amish were everywhere in their black buggies. The quaint-looking women and children in long dresses and bonnets strolled down streets lined with black walnut trees and white picket fences. I remarked to Quinn how so far the countryside was all very charming and nothing like what I expected.

She stared ahead and said nothing. I quietly wondered to myself if she still thought I was some kind of loon.

Three boulders came into view marking the entrance to the preserve, which looked from the main road like nothing more than a crop field gone fallow. No gate. No guard. Just a sign that said "Foxfield Preserve" and a gravel road winding up a small rise, parting the field of waist-high goldenrod, foxtail and Queen Anne's lace. At the top of the hill, a little path was cut through the weeds. Quinn pulled to a stop.

"Don't you ever worry about people coming out here and messing with the graves?" I asked.

"Like grave robbers?" she said, putting the car in park and turning off the key. Flatly, she added: "No."

Climbing out of the Toyota, Quinn rattled off the answers to the questions she's asked all the time. The idea that green burials are not legal comes from the rules of most conventional cemeteries and not, usually, the laws of the state or federal government. Conventional cemeteries, for instance, insist the body must be placed in a vault underground to keep the ground over the casket from collapsing and creating sink holes. Uneven ground makes mowing a bitch (my words). Using a vault, according to Quinn, also allows more bodies to be buried per acre—anywhere from 1,000 to 2,000 in a conventional cemetery.

"We had the land surveyed here to accommodate only one to two hundred," she said, before leading me down the trail and answering, finally, the grave-robber question.

"Digging a grave is a tremendous amount of work," she said.

At Foxfield, graves are dug to a depth of about three-and-a-half feet.

"Six feet under is a myth," she said.

Well, not exactly. As many have before me, I traced the popular phrase to merry old England back during The Great Plague of 1665 when it was, in fact, a law enacted under the belief that burying bodies six feet deep would prevent the spread of the disease. If giving your body back to the earth—composting it, as it were—be your goal, people who study this stuff have concluded that roughly four feet underground and no more is the prime "carcass decay zone." In what is also sometimes called the "microbial zone," oxygen can still circulate, facilitating an amazingly fast rate of decay.

How fast? One study I came across in the November 2006 issue of *BioCycle* reported on the findings of a three-year study commissioned by the Iowa Department of Natural Resources on composting livestock. Buried four feet underground, "periodic excavation and observation of small sections of selected windrows showed that all soft tissues associated with the 1,000 lb (450 kg) carcasses were fully decomposed within four to six months in unturned emergency composting windrows constructed during warm weather, and in eight to ten months in unturned windrows constructed during cold weather."

Ruminate on that for a minute. It's amazing, really. Whether we're talking about cows or humans or even those headline-grabbing fatties you occasionally see on television being hoisted out of their houses on a crane—to think that the re-runs of your sorry predicament could still be playing on *Entertainment Tonight* even as your body, buried in just a couple feet of top soil, were reduced to so much glorious nothing in little less than a year.

But, back to Ohio and the subject of earth removal.

According to Quinn, hand-digging a grave—moving over two tons of loamy clay and rocky Ohio soil—takes a two-man crew anywhere from three to five hours, plus another two to three hours to fill the hole back in. Quinn had never heard of a single instance of grave tampering (or for that matter, of animals digging up a body) on any natural burial preserve in the country, not even America's oldest, the Ramsey Creek Preserve in South Carolina.

"If we found that going on here, we would definitely have to hire guards or something. But honestly, if somebody wanted to steal gold teeth, they could make easier money working at McDonald's."

I've walked through dozens of cemeteries, but there's something eerie about a body-length hump of dirt and knowing there's a corpse underneath.

"What's with the pine needles?" I asked after a moment of silence. A thin layer of old and rust- colored needles covered the heap of chunky clay, rocks and earth.

"Part of the ceremony," Quinn said, adding that the woman under our feet had died of cancer that summer. Quinn remembered how the husband called to purchase the plot, describing his wife as in her forties and an avid gardener who loved the outdoors.

"He came out and selected the site and two or three days later she passed," she said. This particular grave was on the highest point of ground in the preserve and looked out over the fields and woodlots, the autumn hardwoods beginning to color, farm houses and a few scattered barns dotting the surrounding country. A wedge of geese flew over and all around tiger swallowtails, monarchs and dozens of tiny white cabbage butterflies flittered. There were worse spots to spend eternity, I suppose.

We stood a while, then walked back to the road. Quinn described her plans to some day see the entire preserve planted with native Indian grass, big and little blue stem, blazing star. In the lower part of the preserve, Quinn's goal was to convert the field of goldenrod and foxtail into a grove of oak, cherry and poplar.

Down the gravel road we found another fresh grave, much like the first except for a couple of toppled pots of wilted flowers. I asked about grave markers. When the grass grows back, how will people know where their loved ones were buried? Quinn explained that while families have the option of marking a grave with a native tree, flower, plant or flat stone marker, nobody yet had.

It took less than 20 sunny minutes to stroll the perimeter of the preserve. Quinn filled the time with stories: the one about the woman who called to purchase a Foxfield plot for her 50th birthday; how another person who bought a plot stood in the spot and had their picture taken to show friends; and how one man, after planting his flag, plugged the coordinates into his GPS.

"People generally have fun with it," said Quinn. Everyone who buys a plot at Foxfield is given an orange surveyor's flag and invited to walk around until they find a spot that feels right for them. They plant the flag and Quinn later finds the corresponding plot on her map back at the office.

How much does it cost?

Burial plots, Quinn explained, ran $3,200.

Even though I'd just read somewhere that the average cost for a conventional burial plot in the U.S. was around $4,000, I found it pretty staggering.

"Roughly half of that is split between the preserve's endowment care trust and The Wilderness Center," Quinn explained, adding that the price is based on the fact that space at Foxfield is limited, and also that the money provides a guarantee that the property will be maintained in perpetuity.*

Quinn then segued into another story about the Unitarian minister who phoned a couple of months back explaining that he was interested in laying down the cash to buy a plot, but wanted to know if she had a problem with bodies being buried on the grounds without a coffin.

"He wanted to be thrown into a hole with his clothes on," said Quinn. "I told him that would be fine, but had he talked to anyone else about it, mainly his family, who would actually have to carry out the request?"

The man admitted he hadn't.

"He told me he wanted to help change the way people viewed death in this country," said Quinn, adding that she may have talked him out of being buried there. "Sometimes people don't realize, but it [a green burial] is actually a huge undertaking that can be very difficult on the family if they're not totally on board."

I asked Quinn what her burial plans were. Did she plan on being buried at FoxField? She claimed not to have figured

---

* If a cemetery association or company sells internment rights, it is required to set aside at least ten percent of the gross sale proceeds from the sale into an Endowment Care Trust. Only interest from the dividends may be withdrawn for perpetual sale of the cemetery.

it all out yet. Her family was in Pennsylvania. She'd only lived in Ohio since the summer; it didn't yet feel like home.

What was the biggest surprise so far—the most unexpected thing about her job?

"I guess that it turned out to be sadder than I thought it would be. I attend all the funerals here and, I mean, I don't know any of these people. But it's still very sad."

I thought about changing the subject and asking again about digging a grave, but suddenly, I didn't want to anymore. I didn't mention my change of heart to Quinn, but on the way back to The Wilderness Center she mentioned that if I really wanted to dig a grave I could go out in the woods behind the Center's main complex. Rather than trying to explain that suddenly I didn't see the point, I made some excuse.

It wasn't that Quinn told me the effort would probably eat up the rest of that beautiful afternoon. ("With one of the graves we dug this summer, a couple of feet down we hit twenty-inches of limestone and it still took two hours with a track-hoe.") Foxfield was a nice enough place to be buried, but my soul had no connection to the place. I was beginning to realize that in planning my green burial—any burial for that matter—it pays to be flexible, but on this point I was certain: when I die I want my burial place to be more than just a pretty plot of ground. I want to have real ties to the land where I'm buried. I want to know the place so that my body might in death feed the very land that in life sustained my soul.

The Seventh Week

 **Wherein bubbling
blisters are broken,
dirt flies and a big
friggin' hole is formed.**

"You wanna' do what?"

A couple days after returning from Ohio—after, of course, dutifully following the trooper's warning back in Bellevue and getting the Subaru's headlight repaired—I was beginning to wish I'd taken Jennifer Quinn up on letting me dig a mock grave in the woods behind her office.

"You wanna' do what?"

I got more or less the same bewildered reaction from every one of the cemetery operators who bothered to return my call. I might as well have been asking these total strangers if I could pop in at their house for dinner sometime, take their daughter to the drive-in, or something equally untoward.

"Come again?"

After I'd explained anywhere from two to twenty times that I was neither a prospective customer nor a funeral director with an actual body to get in the ground, nobody seemed to want any part of "what I was selling." One cemetery manager actually said this to me. Another cited insurance concerns.

"We have employees specifically trained to do that kind of work."

"Trained?" I said, incredulous. "To dig a hole?"

"It's more complicated than that. There's heavy equipment involved. You know, nobody digs graves by hand anymore."

Finally, I had a woman on the line who actually sounded intrigued by the idea. I made my pitch. At this point, I was ready to modify my original plan—digging a grave that I hoped would actually be used by somebody recently deceased. Now, I simply wanted to gain permission to be there while a real grave was being dug. I figured if I could just get my foot in the door, then maybe during the excavation I could ply the digging crew into letting me jump in the hole and shovel a few scoops to get a feel for the operation.

"Can I give you my name and number?"

"Sure," she said.

"And you'll let me know the next time there's a funeral planned?"

"Sure," she echoed.

Everybody's seen the movie where the desperate parents of the abducted child finally get the ransom call from the sinister kidnappers. A mob of very busy and stern-looking federal agents are always crowded around with their earphones on fixing to trace the call.

The phone rings.

"Just keep him on the line," hisses the steely cop before the distressed parent picks up the phone with a pair of praying hands.

All of a sudden, it felt like that—like the woman on the end was just letting me talk.

"You're never going to call, are you?" I said.

"Mmm, probably not."

"Well, thank you," I said.

"Thank *you*," she said. "Bye, now."

Hard to say that I took anything from this exercise except a growing perception that very few people associated with the conventional funeral industry wanted to speak to me unless there was a possibility to make a buck. I could understand the reservations of the funeral directors and morticians (my aim to observe an actual embalming was also being stymied by unreturned phone calls); after all, I'd always made it clear that I was writing a book about planning a *natural* burial. They certainly had nothing to gain by helping out a writer who, for all they knew, may not be kind to them.

But even some in the green burial crowd were put off by my requests to talk, usually after I directed them to my blog. One such person was a woman from Oregon who took umbrage at my online observation that any American paying $3,000 to have an English Ecopod shipped all the way across the Atlantic by jet or diesel-spewing freighter just maybe didn't have their carbon footprint or the greener interests of planet forefront in their mind. This woman thought my writing "jaded" and "cynical." In an email to my website, after twice mentioning that she was also a writer with a book on natural burial in the works, she made it clear that she didn't appreciate my "snipes" or my "rush to judgment."

"What people want are truthful things that can help them navigate the territory they need to examine," she scolded, "and believe me, if you've got cancer . . . or you're staring down the muzzle of life and it's pointed at you, cynicism rings with a hollow bravado and you know it's a useless ploy that is, at the end of the day, a waste of time. One faces the Maker with facts."

Quite frankly, I was a little surprised. I figured anyone who'd entertain being buried in something that looked more like a kayak than a coffin would at least have a sense of humor.

I've actually known plenty of people stricken with cancer and other terminal maladies—loved ones who, in "staring down the muzzle of life," lost every scrape of human dignity, including being able to go to bathroom by themselves. But I can't remember many who lost their ability to laugh, right up until the end.

I wanted to point out that I wasn't trying to be funny, but if what I write happened to make people laugh while they began to think about their end of life choices, so be it. On the subject of green burial, I wanted to reiterate that I am not an expert, that the purpose of this exercise was to look at green burial with the eyes of an unbiased layman—a regular guy who only wanted a simple, planet-friendly burial one day— the same sort of person the green burial movement needed to reach if the idea was ever to go mainstream.

Then I remembered that many people in this world don't believe there's room for humor or levity when talking about death. If you can't approach the topic with anything other than a trembling lower lip or somber seriousness, there are many who'll automatically assume you've never seen the dear light of life leave the eyes of someone you love, and that certainly you've never been close to death yourself. Let's just say that's a pretty big assumption.

Fringe movements are always populated by people who are . . . well, on the fringe. I had to remind myself that right now, green burial in America is an even smaller fringe movement today than cremation was in the 1970s. In 1975 there were only 425 crematories, and 150,000 cremations, in the United States and Canada, according to the Cremation Association of America. "By 1999, there were 1,468 crematories and 595,617 cremations."

The idea of a green burial in this country is still very young. The green burial movement, in my outsider's perspective, is still in the process of defining and, obviously in the minds of some, defending itself. I wanted to remind my friend in Oregon of this—that I believed there was room right now for everything from pine boxes to Ecopods, from opinions on where the movement is and where it might be headed to strict how-to books written by experts that a person could confidently carry to the gates of heaven when it comes time to meet "the Maker." In the end, I not only thanked her for the comments and criticism but also invited her to tell me more. I never did hear from her again.

Someone who did return my messages—and who wasn't afraid to be quoted by name—was Jerry Leisinger, owner of Bubba's Digging in Sioux Falls, South Dakota. Looking for expert advice from someone experienced at digging graves the old-fashioned way, I found Leisinger's website online and gave him a call.

"I always carry a metal file close and have a putty knife in my back pocket," he said. Despite what some might call a morbid occupation, Leisinger came off as affable, friendly and genuinely glad to share with me everything he'd learned during a lifetime of digging graves, which until as recently as twenty years ago was done almost exclusively by hand.

"The old-time gravediggers, like my grandfather, always kept their tools sharp. The putty knife you use to keep the blade clean. Anytime you get dirt or clay sticking to the shovel blade, scrape that off with the putty knife. It makes a difference."

From 1978 to 1990, Leisinger and his father hand-dug in the neighborhood of 100 graves per year—in any season, any weather—just as his grandparents had done for 55 years before.

"My grandfather got paid ten dollars a grave. When my father and I took over the business, it was fifty dollars, then eventually seventy-five."

I chatted with Leisinger for the better part of an hour and my pen never stopped moving, taking down others bits of advice he offered.

Drink plenty of water: Trying to dig a pit in ground so hard that even the metal scoop of a backhoe bounces off takes endurance, strength and plenty of fluids.

"In South Dakota there's gravel, rocks and white chalky clay in some areas," he said. "The worst digging is always in clay."

On a typical South Dakota summer day—before he, too, employed digging machines to do the lion's share of the dirty work—Leisinger could pick, shovel and scoop a grave thirty-six inches wide, eight feet long, and six feet deep in about four hours. In winter, he said, the same hole with nice clean edges and smooth sides might take anywhere from eight to ten.

In addition to his spade, flat shovel, pick and ax (for neatly marking the perimeter of the grave site and chopping out tree roots encountered on the way down), in winter Leisinger also employed a contraption called the "grave thawer."

"Picture a metal barrel cut in half—like the hood [of a truck] that spans the length and width of the grave," he said. Wood fire in the old days and later, propane, provided the heat needed to thaw the ground.

Unlike at Foxfield, Leisinger adhered to the "six feet under" rule. Why?

"To accommodate the coffin and the burial vault," he said, adding that the depth of a grave (while only three and a half feet in most natural burial preserves where no concrete vaults are used) is also determined by the frost line.

"Just as the pressure of winter frost pushes up rocks in a farmer's field every year," he said, "the same thing can happen to a vault over time."

According to Leisinger, digging a grave six feet deep also keeps at bay scavenging and burrowing animals, which in South Dakota meant gophers and badgers, pesky varmints that have no reservations about making a home out of wooden coffins buried in shallow ground.

One last bit of advice: Carry a yardstick.

"The width of a grave is just as important as depth," warned Leisinger. "Start digging at one end of the grave and work your way across, end to end, ten inches at a time," he said. "On the day of the funeral when the family is there saying their final goodbyes to the deceased, you definitely want to make sure the latter fits neatly in the hole."

Back in Michigan, the week winding down, I had come to a point of frustration. If I was ever going to experience what it was like to dig a grave, then I was going to have to do it on my own piece of land. Trouble is, I'm one of the 150 million people in this country who doesn't have any land.

"After World War II, moving to the suburbs was a key component of the American Dream of upward mobility," reads a September 2004 report in the online version of *The Nation*. "Indeed, the proportion of Americans who live in suburbs has grown steadily, from 23 percent in 1950 to 50 percent in 2000."

Ever since my father died and the farm sold at auction, I've more or less lived in the suburbs. Never more than half an hour from a city of some sort. Never without electricity or indoor plumbing. For someone who used to fancy himself a junior Jeremiah Johnson, this is a hard thing to admit. I know how to plant a garden, pluck a chicken, buck up a cord of firewood, brain-tan an animal hide and shit in woods. Someday I hope to have a bona fide "Back Forty," some place in the woods where I can live more simply. Some place with a little writing cabin on it, a piece of paradise with a meadow and maybe a mountain or two, a trout stream, surrounded by endless acres of forest filled with wild solitude and, need I say, oodles of bears, birds, mountain lions and big-antlered game. (Think Walden and Sand County and then send photos, property description, and written applications: I'm accepting donations.) It would also have to be in a state where the law would allow for my body to be buried on the land after spending a lifetime learning from and loving it.

Like half the people in America, I've spent most of my life moving from house to house, suburb to suburb, living right alongside a parade of faceless neighbors I've never bothered to get to know. It's a trend most continue after death. And, to me, that's very, very sad. I'd rather be buried alone—Abbey style—in a place yet to be determined then spend forever in a cemetery surrounded by strangers.

That's why private family cemeteries have always intrigued me. I bought a first edition of Lisa Carlson's book *Caring for the Dead*—an overwhelmingly informative book that Carlson obviously had ample time and, I assume, discretionary income to complete—and was pleasantly surprised to find that all of my favorite states—from Montana to Michigan—allow for the setting up of a private family plot. Basically, any state with a lot of woods and farm country, or any state that allows for things like driving over 55 on the highway, or driving around town with your deer rifle clearly hanging from a rack in the back window of a pickup, probably has provisions for burial on private land.

Take Michigan, for example. Carlson gave a most succinct synopsis of private burial law:

> *Family graveyards under one acre outside city or village limits are permissible. Such land is exempt from taxation and must be recorded with the county clerk. You need to get permission from the local health department first. A sensible guideline is 150 ft. from any water or water supply, 25 ft. from a power line, and don't get too close to the property line. Draw a map of your land showing where it will be and, once approved by the health department, pay to have the map recorded with your deed.*

I currently live on a lot just shy of an acre, a woodsy little cul-de-sac with a strip of hardwoods—a "nature corridor"—out back. Where could I dig? An alternative was to strike out on public property. In Michigan there are over a million acres of forested public land, but you can't just go out there with a spade and a shovel and start digging holes. Maybe I could find a bit of abandoned property that wasn't posted "No Trespassing." I could dig a hole there, and then (of course) cover it up and leave without a trace.

How much trouble could a person get into doing that, you might wonder?

Apparently, a whole hell of a lot.

I'm referring to an Associated Press article from earlier in the year with a headline that read, "Oregon man digs hole that looks like grave, gets arrested."

According to the January 2008 Washington County Sheriff's memo that inspired the story, authorities received a 911 call from the caretaker of a private property who claimed to be "holding a man at gunpoint after finding him digging a hole."

The hole-digger turned out to be 63-year-old Ronald Karel who innocently claimed to be "looking for evidence of Mt. St. Helen's ash." While the report does not give specific details as to what went through the minds of the deputies called to the scene, presumably a piercing squint and collective wide-eyed utterance of that phrase I knew well—"Come again?"—is not a stretch. I'm guessing here, but Karel might as well have told them he was a writer doing research for a book on planning his own green burial.

Further investigation revealed that Karel had, indeed, been digging a hole. The hole measured six feet long, three feet deep, and varied between two and a half and three feet wide. "Experienced detectives believed it could be a grave site," which proved enough to book and hold Karel in the county clink on charges of criminal trespass and criminal mischief. Because of "the suspicious nature of the hole," Karel's bond was set at $20,000, while police went looking for a victim. They sent out a call to relatives, friends and associates of Karel's to come forward if they had been harmed or felt they might be in danger if he were released.

I thought I was willing to do just about anything to dig my own grave, except jail time. So, early on Friday morning, after the wife went off to work and the children to preschool—and, it must be said, all my neighbors tootled off to their real jobs—I went the only route open to me by striking off across the yard and into the wood line with all the tools kind Jerry Leisinger had recommended.

I found the work wonderfully taxing. After taking my double-bitted ax and hacking up the dimensions of the pit, I raked off the leaves and placed them in a pile to one side of a blue tarp I'd laid out in a neat square to put the soil on. Michigan soil is rich and sandy and, at least where I was lucky enough to dig, all but devoid of rocks. Working from end to end, ten inches down at every pass, as Leisinger had instructed, only occasionally did I have to swap my spade for an ax to hack away roots. I confess I only stopped the excavation once for a sip of water. The pile of dirt outside my hole grew larger by the minute under a pluming shower of earth, one shovel-full every three to five seconds. I kept thinking that if someday my friends were to dig my grave, they'd be relieved to find my backyard so amiable to digging. Streaked with yellow and orange, the soil cut like custard, shovel- after shovel-full, until less than three hours after breaking ground I was standing well past my waist in a perfectly shaped grave.

I'd had a hell of a time. I'd gotten so into the work that I'd gone four-and-a-half-feet down when I was only planning to excavate three. I knew I was out of my depth, as it were, when I stopped finding bugs and red worms and the heads of grubs poking out of the soil on the walls of my grave. I've said this before, but any grave more than four feet deep is for people who aren't interested in their bodies doing anything other than decomposing into a cloud of methane and putrid sludge. Aerobic decomposition—the thing that enriches the soil, fattens the worms and helps push up the daisies—happens only if a body is buried in topsoil. So I filled a little back into the hole, climbed out and stood aside to admire the work.

Something didn't feel right.

It didn't have anything to do with my stinging palms. I simply expected to get more—something emotionally significant or revealing—out of the operation than a couple of bubbling blisters and the pleasant feeling of muddy, muscle-weary fatigue you can only get after moving a couple tons of earth. On the one hand, I was proud of "my grave." I had my wife take my picture standing in the thing when she got home. On the other hand—and this had been nagging at me since I got it in my head that the exercise was somehow necessary—what was the point of digging a hole of these dimensions unless it was to bury something?

Loving stories about pirates and any sort of subterranean adventure when I was little, I remember digging random holes in the backyard hoping to discover gold buried in a treasure chest. I was the kid who, after hearing about how China is on the opposite side of the world, once tried for a week to dig through two feet of Pennsylvania shale to get there. But 30 years later, what was I digging for? I wasn't looking for evidence of volcanic eruption, like Mr. Karel out there in Washington. I wasn't trying to bury anything for real. What was I doing?

After my wife snapped a photo, I think my young son, Gabe, summed it up best.

"That's a pretty big hole, Dad."

And for the next two hours, filling the thing back in, that's pretty much what I thought, too: without anything to bury, that's all it was. Nothing special. Nothing sacred. Just a big, friggin' hole.

The Eighth Week

 Wherein a family's obligation to a deceased loved one is questioned and the work of a death midwife is briefly explored.

My wife put up with the teetering stack of burial books on our nightstand. She never mentioned the charge for coffin plans on the credit card, the "death calls" at dinnertime, me excavating a gigantic pit on the edge of the yard or the growing and uncanny knack I'd developed for bringing every one of our conversations around to the subject of my burial.

"Honey, look at the snow falling outside. It's so beautiful."

"Yeah, wow. But *brrrr!* I bet the ground's as hard as concrete. Can you imagine trying to dig my grave right now?"

Or . . .

"Did my mother leave a message about us going home for Christmas?"

"She did and, you know, we had the most interesting conversation. Did you know she remembers being a little girl and having a home funeral for your great-grandfather? And then her father, too. That's something I'd really like to look into."

In this manner we talked about our burial plans without ever talking about our burial plans. I found this odd given that every other life-defining decision up to that point—getting married, having children, where to school those children—involved long and careful deliberation—and, where the subject of a second child was concerned, $50-an-hour psychiatric counsel to help me wrap my mind around the idea. For all these things, we looked also for input from friends and family. And then there was the unasked-for advice.

When Nancy was pregnant and showing with our first, I was amazed at how often complete strangers would approach, sometimes going so far as to reach out and, without asking, touch her globular middle. The bigger she became, the bolder everyone got.

"Whoa! You're huge!"

Nancy and I used to talk about how little compunction—especially in those final months—people showed about asking her flat-out to pull up her shirt and show them how big she really was. At parties we'd meet people who, instead of shaking hands, would reach out to grope my wife's midsection before proffering advice on everything from breastfeeding to the best way to keep our marriage from tanking in those maddening months after bringing the newborn home.

"Make sure to make time for each other," they'd say, or, "Go on a date at least once a month."

I wondered what it would be like if people were so open with one another about dying. Instead of looking the other way when an ashy old person was being wheeled down the sidewalk with an oxygen tank, we'd exclaim, "Wow! You look like you're on the way out. Are you thinking cremation or a more traditional burial?"

Where birth was concerned we listened to everybody. Then we talked about everything we'd heard or read, and we listened to each other. But the subject of death and burial had never come up in all the years of our marriage. Now, however, it flowed into the conversation casually, say while driving in the car or chatting over Friday night cocktails in the kitchen while the children tumbled around upstairs out of earshot. I'd ask her how her week went. Then she'd ask me about mine and that would invariably lead into something I'd read—some morbid factoid about human decomposition or environmental concerns related to conventional cremation and burial.

"Did you know that the EPA doesn't regulate emissions from crematories?" I'd say.

"*Should* I have known that?" she'd reply.

"The EPA estimates that anywhere from six hundred pounds of mercury come out of crematories in the United States every year from—get this—dental fillings!"

"That doesn't really sound like a lot."

"Yes, well . . . think about your carbon footprint, dear. Have you ever considered all the energy it takes to run one of those ovens?"

Figures on this point varied. But the general consensus was that an electric- or natural gas-fired cremation oven used about 2,000 cubic feet of energy to incinerate one cadaver, producing as much CO_2—about 250 pounds—as our happily average American home produces in one week.

"Can't I plant trees or something to offset that?"

"Well, I suppose."

I should probably mention here that traditional cremation might not be the greenest way to go, but it's still better than conventional burial for the simple reason that cremation is a once-and-done deal. You can find sources that will say cremation releases into the air everything from carbon monoxide to cancer-causing formaldehyde fumes from people who also have their bodies embalmed first for the purposes of a public viewing. I also found figures that said that the energy required to incinerate one body was equal to the fuel needed to drive a car 4,800 miles, which is why when somebody asked me if cremation wasn't considered green, my quick answer was "no," even though I sometimes felt as if the reasons why amounted to environmental nitpicking.

In our house, Nancy has always been the more practical and traditional when it comes to matters of ritual circumstance. Despite the information on mercury and carbon emissions from cremated corpses, she actually liked the idea of a scorching, 1,600-degree, oven-baked immolation. That's what she wanted for herself.

We don't always agree on everything.

Early on, for instance, I offhandedly mentioned that I absolutely did not want to be embalmed and then put on display so all my friends could stand around whispering about how peaceful I looked. Only an occasional church-goer, I couldn't see myself wanting a full-blown church service either. My wife, on the other hand—while she, too, wasn't interested in either embalming or an open casket— said a church service conducted by a minister who actually knew her was exactly what she wanted done.

Nancy has generally been supportive of just about every lamebrain, off-kilter, wacked-out thing I've ever expressed interest in doing in life. But in burial—at least when it came to the early discussions of what her role would be in mine— she had a couple of looming concerns:

"Are you going to ask me to remember you by hiking to the top of a mountain to kill an elk with a spear or something?" she asked one day during a conversation about our daughter's college fund—a morphed conversation that started as a socio-economic-philosophical discussion about why parents are expected to pay for their children's education in the first place and how this unwritten and, as far as I was concerned, unreasonable parental obligation made it increasingly unlikely that I would ever be able to be buried on our own property.

Another of her concerns was my growing interest in home funerals.

As a couple, we'd bucked convention before. For instance, when most of our friends were taking the better part of a year to plan lavish weddings that ultimately cost more than the GDP of the Polynesian island nation of Tuvalu, we opted for a simple ceremony at home: a very small, intimate affair with only immediate family and a few close friends. We've talked about homeschooling our children. For the birth of our oldest, Gabe, we went the route of a midwife in the belief that it would be the best way to deliver "naturally." We even talked about a full-blown home birth—rubber sheets, incense and a CD in the background playing soothing sounds and the songs of humpback whales.

So why not a home funeral?

"It's just not me," Nancy said, reminding me of the time Gabe slipped in the kitchen and split his chin open on the jagged corner of the open dishwasher door. Rivulets of blood slid down his little neck and Nancy got weak-kneed and almost passed out.

"I mean, what about the smell? And, you know . . . don't things leak out of a person when they're dead? What am I supposed to do about *that*?"

There's nothing written that says a home funeral is necessary to designate your burial "green," but there's definitely something more "organic" about it. At least to my way of thinking, it's certainly the most intimate and personal way to mark the passing of someone dear. In all but a handful of states, taking care of a loved one from "last breath to final resting place," without any involvement from a funeral director, is totally legal.

But, I found, the laws in a handful of states can be tricky. For example, here in Michigan, a family can undertake a home funeral as long as they hire a funeral director to "certify" the death certificate and "supervise" the disposition of the body. I didn't yet understand what these vagaries meant, but Nancy made it clear that if I wanted a home funeral—while it wasn't totally out of the question—I would probably have to first find a death midwife.

I actually met two sorts of death midwives during the weeks exploring my green burial options. One kind is present during the final hours of a person's dying to create a sacred space and help the dying transition, or be "reborn" into the next life—the life after death, if you believe in that sort of thing.

But when most people talk about a death midwife, what they're referring to is somebody who assists the family of the deceased in conducting a home funeral. A death midwife is to a home funeral what a doula is to a home birth. They help with a lot of the heavy lifting, literally, by facilitating the transport of the body from the hospital to the home, and from the home to the burial place. They help the family with the paperwork that goes along with dying and—to facilitate the wake or home ritual—they know how to care for an unembalmed body.

Just as most people once knew how to can vegetables, milk a cow, butcher a pig and manage a home birth, caring for an unembalmed dead body at home was fairly common knowledge less than a hundred years ago. When my mother-in-law was a girl back in Perry County, Pennsylvania, her family had home funerals in the house and hotel they owned until almost 1950. Now it's called an "art"—the art of death midwifery—and it's practiced by relatively few nationwide.

"I'm a white German / Russian—a white chick who likes African drums."

I'd called Reverend Rebekah Benner of Akron, Ohio, after having no luck locating a death midwife anywhere near my home in northern Michigan. Jennifer Quinn of Foxfield Preserve had passed along Benner's name as someone who had worked with the family of the first person buried there in the summer of 2008. I wanted to ask Benner about the experience, and also figured she was the most likely source for locating a death midwife closer to me. While she knew of death midwives working in California, Washington, Pennsylvania and Virginia, no one in Michigan came to her mind.

We ended up chatting anyway, after Benner told me about her cabin in Michigan's Upper Peninsula. She also told me that she was into crystals and new age religion. After I'd called and left a message for her earlier in the week, she'd even looked up my website and read my green burial blog. She thought what I'd written was great, or something to that effect. Of course, I commended her sense of humor and fine literary taste before asking how, exactly, someone wakes up one day and decides they'd like to become a death midwife.

One of those energetic and charitable individuals I occasionally run into who make me feel like a totally selfish slug, Benner casually rattled off a résumé of selfless giving and religious service so long my pen could barely keep up. Minister. Sunday school teacher. Hospice volunteer. Grief recovery counselor. In a later email, I had to ask her to help untangle my notes.

"I'm a licensed minister, affiliated with the Unitarian Universalist Church and I [just] completed the course work in Volunteer Pastoral Care with SUMMA hospitals, [as well as] Akron General Medical Center's 'Advanced Spiritual Healthcare' program to become a volunteer pastoral care chaplain," she clarified.

When not working full-time as an office manager for an Akron area "architectural/engineering/planning firm," Benner said she can often be found visiting hospital patients, conducting meditation classes ("I studied with Kwang Jang Nym and Stephen Coates of the Koryo MooSool Association's Center for Spiritual Formation to earn certification as a meditation facilitator") or leading grief-recovery sessions for families dealing with death.

"On any weekend I may have a meditation class scheduled on Saturday morning, see someone who needs a grief-recovery session or spiritual guidance, then a drum circle benefit at church in the evening—I'm the 'official' drummer for the First Congregational Church of Akron Labyrinth. I play an awesome metal hang drum from Switzerland!"

Turning the conversation back to death midwifery, I had a couple questions for Brenner. How do you know if a home funeral is for you? And what if your spouse or family member isn't exactly on board? Benner answered by way of a story.

"Last summer, the husband—I'll call him John—of the first person buried at Foxfield called. He said his wife was dying and that she wanted a home funeral."

Benner always does first what she calls a "phone intake."

"It's a list of questions," she explained. "Is this your will? Are the wishes in writing? Who has power of attorney? Who will be involved?" Benner described that the goal of the initial phone call was to see if the person on the other end of the line had really considered everything that a home funeral means.

"Have you told your friends and family? What about cleansing the body and moving the body. Is this something they can handle? Or is it too *icky*?"

The questions she asked were refreshingly frank. The calls, Benner said, usually last over an hour.

"Where will the body be in the house? Do you have a religious preference?"

Benner's fee for a phone consultation and, later, coming to the client's house and talking with the family is $100.

"I really don't like calling them 'clients,'" she said. "But at the house I will look at the layout to see if it's even possible to move a body from upstairs to downstairs. It takes four people or more to move a body. Six is actually ideal."

Benner's had at least one case where every arrangement was made only to have family members get nervous and back out.

"What do you think the obligation of a spouse and family is to honor the last request of the deceased?"

"That's a tough question," she said. "I believe funerals are both for the dead and the living. So maybe there needs to be a compromise between the last wishes of the dead and what the living can handle, especially if the living are going to harbor guilt for not carrying out a person's wishes. Funerals are about the dead person's life, but with their passing it becomes the story of the living . . . and for the family and friends of the loved one, a funeral becomes a rite of passage. We plan for birth. We plan for marriage. But most people don't plan for death—their own funeral—which is our last act on Earth."

The Ninth Week

 **Wherein the question of where to buy dry ice is answered and more on the art of a death midwife is learned.**

Death midwife Nora Cedarwind Young tells a story:

"A couple years ago," she begins, "I went to help an old woman with a home funeral for her husband. They were married a long time—their whole life, if I remember."

The woman was helping during what Young calls "the ritual bathing of a body." Just as a newborn is cleansed before being swaddled in a clean blanket and handed off to his mother to begin the journey into life, for most of recorded history the dead have been lovingly prepared for the journey into the afterlife in much the same way. Unlike the unemotional, sterilizing scrub-down given corpses by an undertaker prior to embalming, a bath becomes a final and symbolic act of love when performed by those closest to the deceased. In a familiar, comfortable setting, where there are no strangers and no time constraints, it's a chance for the living to begin coming to terms with the reality of a loved one's passing.

Bathing the man's body with soapy water scented with flowery oils, Young remembered how neither she nor the old woman said a word until halfway through the process when the midwife noticed the woman take up the hand of her husband and begin to weep.

"Which, of course, is not unusual," Young recalls. "Except, in this case the woman was smiling a little bit, too. He had cancer, I think."

But, says Young, that's not the point.

The husband had been sick for many months and his wife had cared for him. Now the man was dead and his wife, aside from a few tears, appeared more than a little at peace with it.

"She looked over at me and said she was so happy. I remember the husband lying there and he had that delicate, paper-thin skin the dying can get toward the end. She told me that this was the first time in almost a year that she had been able to touch him without causing him great pain."

When I asked Young, *Why a home funeral? Why go to all the trouble?*, this was the anecdote she told before answering my questions with a question of her own: *We care for our loved ones when they're living, so why not care for them when they're dead?*

"More than anything, a home funeral is about the healing that's facilitated by the hands-on, physical contact with our beloved dead," Young says. "I'm still in touch with many of the people I've helped through this process, and I'm always humbled and amazed by the ones who have written or called or come up to me years later to tell me the experience was one of the most beautiful in their lives. It's empowering [for the living] to be a part of those final actions."

I came to call on Young at the suggestion of death midwife Rebekah Benner, after my questioning turned to the pointed specifics of dealing with human bodies after death. Benner had learned death midwifery from Young during a long weekend workshop, what Benner described as an experience both wonderful and intense.

Even before my talk with Benner, I had been picking up and reading anything I could find about naturally caring for the dead at home. Anybody interested in this kind of thing eventually comes to know the name Jerrigrace Lyons.

Every article and biography I read about Lyons credited her with founding the modern death midwifery movement and reinventing the "long lost concept of the American home funeral." As the story goes, twelve years ago, Lyons accidentally discovered death midwifery after helping to carry out the last wishes of her close friend Carolyn Whiting. Whiting had died suddenly, but not before directing specifically that she wanted loved ones to bathe and dress her unembalmed body, and then celebrate together in an intimate home memorial before each taking a portion of her ashes and scattering them "around the world."

"The privacy of Carolyn's home lent itself to creating a sacred and intimate atmosphere in which to express all the emotions—grief, pain, love and even joy—that washed like waves over our souls, helping us to cope with and accept the death of our precious friend," Lyons told Bill Strubble, a writer for the online magazine *Common Ground*. Lyons founded her business, Final Passages, and has since helped families in close to 300 home funerals, mostly in Oregon and California where her non-profit company is based.

On her website, Final Passages.org, I found that Lyons regularly lectured and conducted three-day workshops (Levels 1 and 2, at $375 per level) covering everything from "what to have in your home funeral midwifery kit" to "hands-on techniques" to "moving and carrying a body." For around $1,000, Lyons could be hired by a family to personally help with the washing, clothing and conducting of a home wake for a loved one recently departed. Or, for those with less means and more of a do-it-yourself spirit, they could purchase Lyons' complete guidebook online—*Creating Home Funerals*—for about 50 bucks.

Is conducting a home funeral really as simple as following a step-by-step tutorial in a book? From what I uncovered, it seems as if everybody except licensed funeral directors think so. When it comes to the washing, the sheet changing, dressing and watchful attention given the body during the actual wake, the process of caring for the dead is most commonly likened to taking care of a helpless infant or a bedridden invalid.

"You could produce a training manual in three sentences: Keep it cool. Wash it. Pop it in a box," wrote the United Kingdom's Charles Cowling on his blog, "The Good Funeral Guide." "An undertaker doesn't do anything that you couldn't, in a way that a plumber, say, almost certainly can. The dead are wholly safe in the hands of amateurs so long as they (the amateurs) are up for it, for there's nothing you can do to a dead body in a well-intentioned way which that dead body will actually mind."

Nora Cedarwind Young has herself helped conduct over two dozen home funerals since the mid-90s. During our phone interview, she stressed more than once that she doesn't handle the home funeral alone. "I only direct or 'assist' the family," she said. "It's very important you note that." Over the years, she's written dozens of articles on everything from planning a green burial to how to write your own obituary.

We chatted for the better part of an hour and I found her wonderfully candid on everything having to do with her work . . . especially when the subject turned to the most common questions she's asked about home funerals.

"After the is-it-even-legal question, people want to know about how you actually care for the beloved dead at home."

(Young uses terms like *beloved dead*, that coming from anyone else probably would have struck me as put-on and contrived.) There's abdominal purging, for instance. "When the death is natural, the human body actually has a beautiful way of shutting down. They stop eating. They stop taking fluids. But sometimes the body does do a little purge after death. So before the sacred bathing you have to press on the abdominal area to remove any air or digested matter."

To hear her talk, so enchantingly calm and matter-of-fact, it was easy to forget what she was talking *about*. Snapping back to reality, I tried to imagine my wife—a woman who, like her mother, I swear has never so much as broken wind in her life—pushing shit and farts out of my cold and withered corpse.

"Not everyone is going to be a good candidate for a home funeral," Young said. "One person can't do it alone." In fact, it takes at minimum three. Maybe more if after the wake the body has to be carried down, for instance, a long flight of stairs. If narrow hallways, sharp corners and several flights of stairs prevent the deceased from being carried outside in a coffin, Young will tie the hands and arms across the chest to keep them from snagging on door jams and generally flopping around.

I pictured the body, stiff with rigor mortis at this point, being stood up like a refrigerator or a cigar store Indian to make a tight corner, but Young explained that it wasn't like that at all. A person might die with the eyes open, or the mouth agape, but there's a window of time before rigor mortis sets in. By the time the wake is over, the body has softened and become malleable again.

"Coins on the eyes used to be heavy enough to hold the lids closed. Now I'll use rocks, round river stones, for instance, or even Super Glue. I'll use a roll of toilet paper under the jaw. Or I'll tie a scarf around the jaw and pull it up to set it in that position before rigor mortis sets in."

After the ritual bathing and while the jaw and eyes "set," she and the family might prepare the dry ice. Where do you get dry ice? Grocery stores, meat markets, fish vendors and even WalMart sell it.

"It takes about thirty- to forty-dollars worth for a four or five-day funeral," said Young, who wraps pieces of ice in brown grocery bags, then places them discreetly out of sight under the covers—two pieces side-by-side under chest and lower back to help cool and slow the decomposition of the body's major organs.

In her death midwife "travel kit," Young carries items such as medical gloves, adult diapers, nail clippers, alcohol, dry shampoo and make-up. There's also an X-Acto knife, a suturing kit and Krazy Glue if, as she is sometimes called to do, the preparation of a body includes closing up any minor wounds.

After the stones on the eyes and the scarf around the jaw are removed, Young told me how her job becomes mostly about creating and maintaining a "sacred space."

"The ambiance of the room is very important," she says. "I might play some soft music, build an altar with a candle and a picture of the beloved dead, any precious belongings, maybe a flower floating in water."

While death certificates are signed, Young describes scenes of families sitting around telling stories about the deceased, or children and parents doing art or writing final messages on the wooden coffin or cardboard cremation container.

"Unlike the sterile experience of a conventional funeral, you're not at the mercy of a funeral director's schedule during a home funeral. People come and go, paying their respects and spending as much time with the beloved dead as they need. You get more of a chance for conversation and laughter at a home funeral, which—I know it's cliché—but it really is the best medicine ... Most people today know more about assembling a stereo or computer than they do about what is necessary to facilitate the death of a loved one," she said, before interjecting another old saying about death and taxes.

"People always say these things are sure things in life. But whereas we talk about taxes all the time, we don't talk about death. I believe people would be better off if they started having these conversations, and a home funeral is a place where that can happen. But in the end—a home funeral, a green or even conventional burial—I don't really care what people choose. I care that they make a choice that is good and right for them."

The Tenth Week

 **Wherein issues of privacy thwart efforts to observe the embalming of an actual human cadaver.**

So I thought it would be easy to wrangle permission from a funeral home or a mortuary college to sit in and watch a cadaver get embalmed. I mean, why not? Thousands of people donate their bodies to be used for scientific and academic study. And the director of Wayne State University's Mortuary Science program in Detroit told me that, sure enough, they used actual human cadavers to teach students the process.

"Great. So when can I come down and observe?"

A written explanation that my interest was scholarly and that I wasn't some kind of kook (trust me on this) was followed by a couple weeks of unreturned phone calls. Unambiguous rejection finally came in the form of an email from "Instructor of Embalming" Sharon Lynn Gee:

"Due to policy, I cannot accommodate your request. The privilege to view and participate in an embalming is reserved for registered Mortuary Science students only."

That, as they say, was that.

So I began working other angles, starting with the owner of the funeral home in Pennsylvania who took care of the traditional cremation and internment of my father-in-law two years ago. While I sat back and waited for the reply that never came, I thought about the possibility of weaseling my way into actually working at a funeral home for a spell. But what kind of job? Washing hearses? Dusting floor model caskets and cremation urns? And who would hire me—a shifty, middle-aged guy with a sketchy job history, a notebook in his pocket and twitchy ink-stained fingers? What was my motivation? What was my story?

"So, Bob. Tell me. Why do you want to work at Mortensen Funeral Home?"

"To tell the truth, I don't. What I'd really like to do is hide out in the chemical closest and catch an embalming after I mop the floor. Whaddya' say?"

That probably wasn't going to work.

On a tip from my doctor, after I complained during my annual physical that no one would talk to me, I called local funeral director Gary Mortensen and asked him flat out if I could come in and watch him embalm somebody.

"Business has been slow," he quipped. "The economy is so bad people don't want to die. They can't afford it."

Mortensen, in what has always been a family-operated business, owns three funeral homes in northern Michigan—one each in Bellaire, Central Lake and Mancelona. In spite of claiming to not understand why suddenly everybody was interested in green burials—"It's not like it's a new idea or anything"—he was at least sympathetic to what I was trying to do.

"Have you tried the mortuary college?" he asked.

I told him I had.

"I wish I could help you," Mortensen said. "But here's what you'd have to do . . . ."

To observe Mortensen work—or any private funeral director, for that matter—I would have to first get permission from the deceased's family. I told my editor about this sticky little problem.

"Can you imagine making that call? I'd rather get embalmed myself." I laughed out loud.

"So do it," she deadpanned.

I naturally assumed she meant track down a grieving family, but now, come to think of it . . . .

At this point, I was used to asking bizarre questions. But more macabre and awkward territory I could not imagine trying to negotiate. Would Mortensen—a man with 30 years experience talking to complete strangers about the pain and grossly uncomfortable business of what to do with a loved one's remains—do me the favor by broaching the subject with the next sobbing somebody who came through his doors? Or, at least, maybe slide the next of kin my card between the Kleenex?

I didn't think so. His reply came back with words more or less to that effect. Mortensen sounded like an affable, accommodating fellow. But, understandably, not even "affable" and "accommodating" was enough to help me.

I once stopped taking my dog to a veterinarian who had a policy that no customer was allowed in the room during an examination of their pet. After all, I won't take my car to a mechanic who won't let me stand in the garage while he's clanking around under the hood. All kidding aside, while on the one hand I totally understand and respect and would never want to violate the privacy of a deceased individual or a grieving family, the closed-door policy at Wayne State, whose purpose on this Earth is to teach this stuff, bothered me, even though . . . even though the truth is I've never had any intention of having my own remains embalmed and I seriously doubted that seeing the operation firsthand would change that. To be blunt, the process in my mind was too much like taxidermy. And, although I am a passionate fisherman and a hunter of wild game, I have never been into mounting the head of an animal I killed on the wall—anymore than I would want someone I love embalmed solely for the purposes of putting them temporarily on display.

Webster defines taxidermy as "the process of preparing, stuffing, and mounting the skins of animals" while an embalmer "treats a dead body so as to protect from decay." Taxidermy is said to be a process that preserves an object's "meaning" or memory, rather than its actual "form." The end result of embalming—based on firsthand observation of a father, grandmother, aunts, uncles, a high school friend, an old boss—has always left me feeling that the art of the embalmer and the taxidermist is so similar as to be nearly the same. I'm not alone in making that comparison.

"The Italians, for example, translate embalmer as taxidermist, as no other word or concept even exists in that language. Even in parts of Britain, itself, embalming is seen as a rather barbaric 'tarting up' of the corpse and completely ridiculous," wrote James H. Bedino, a chemist and Director of Research for The Champion Company in a quirky and at times bizarre paper entitled, "Formaldehyde Exposures in Embalming: For Whom the Toxic Bell Tolls." And, it was beginning to look like a book was the closest I was going to get to a mortuary.

So, I read about the principles and practices of embalming in my copy of the book by the same name. Step by every academic and coldly detached step—"pack the orifices . . . nostrils, mouth, ears, anus, and vagina . . . . In those cases where the eyeball is completely sunken, the hypodermic injection of massage cream or tissue builder behind and directly into the eyeball will raise and inflate it to its normal contour . . . "—the book contained section and chapter titles like "Influence of Refrigeration on Embalming," "Transient Rigidity," and "Cadaveric Spasms and You." Actually, I made that last one up.

Try reading over 300-plus pages of this stuff—how to shave the body to enhance the effect of cosmetics, how to punch a hole through a cadaver's mandibles for the purposes of wiring a slack jaw shut (a "dental tie" in the vernacular), how to suture or "pin the lips"—and I can tell you it certainly helps to have a sense of humor, which I managed to maintain pretty well until it came to the not-so-subtle violence a mortician must employ in the process of "cavity aspiration."

According to the text, cavity aspiration is necessary " . . . to remove as much of the liquid and semi-solid contents of the viscera . . . to remove gases and liquids [and] prevent purge and flushing . . . to remove blood which has accumulated in the heart and major truck veins . . . ." Plainly speaking, pumping formaldehyde into the veins of a cadaver and then massaging it into every fingertip and toe does not completely pickle a corpse. Every cadaver has a trunk full of innards that must be "aspirated," which the mortician accomplishes with a two-foot long, bayonet-like instrument called the trocar.

With the exception of the opening chapter in Mark Harris's *Grave Matters*, every textbook description I could find that outlined the use of the trocar failed to convey how truly ghastly this phase of the embalming process is. The trocar is driven upward into the cadaver's guts (if you've ever seen video of a plastic surgeon siphoning fat from under the epidermis of an overweight patient, you get the picture) at a point near the navel. The mortician then must repeatedly thrust the instrument into every recess of the ribcage and abdomen, puncturing the heart, the lungs, the stomach, intestines and every major organ. "With an audible sucking sound," writes Harris, "the trocar vacuums up the visceral matter it liberates with each puncture: congested blood, accumulated fluid and gases, fecal matter, urine, the semi-digested hamburger and fries Jenny ate for her final dinner, and masses of bacteria."

Now, if that's not enough to turn you into a hybrid-driving, card-carrying member of the green burial movement, there's always the Internet.

Sharon Lynn Gee, the kindly Wayne State instructor, would not endorse any videos available to the public online. But she did mention one produced by the National Geographic Society and the Cincinnati College of Mortuary Science, the oldest mortuary school in the nation. Roughly three minutes long—featuring classroom scenes and interviews with happy, handsome young morticians-in-training—it struck me as a sanitized, made-for-television infomercial for the trade.

On the other end of the spectrum, a video not mentioned by Ms. Gee, was an eleven-minute, 16mm black and white art house film called, *Thanatopraxie: Der Letzte Weg*. No narration, no music, and certainly not the kind of over-the-shoulder medical documentary you're liable to see late at night on The Discovery Channel.

I watched it early one morning, first thing, when my wife and children were still tucked in their beds asleep. Sitting down to the computer, periodically checking and rechecking over my shoulder to make sure the door to my office was closed, I felt as if the entire exercise was not only unseemly but downright obscene. Everything I'd read about was right there.

Of course, one of the corrupting aspects of television is the illusion that as we sit there watching something play out on the screen, sipping coffee, we are having an actual experience. I could imagine the steely clink of a bloody scalpel on the tray after the mortician cut a slit in the jugular of the old man on the table, the cold, putty-like feel of his skin, the hum of the florescent lights overhead. I could imagine the toxic smell of the room. I could almost imagine being there, maybe finding that one thing that makes it real, that something you hear people talk about later when asked, "So what was it like?"

"You know," I might start, taking on an earnest, thoughtful tone, "at one point I caught a glimpse of the man's hands and I saw a little tan line and around the base of his ring finger where a wedding band must have been . . . ."

But there was none of that. In fact, there was no emotion whatsoever other than the lingering and confounding sense of "why." On the one hand, I found it hard to impugn the undertaker's profession, which I truly believe provides a valuable service to people who need it. Until I have any direct conversation or experience to the contrary, I will believe the majority of those called to this kind of work do so out of a sense of compassion and respect for the dead.

At the same time I couldn't help but think that I was watching an archaic, institutionalized and arguably unnecessary operation (except in cases in which the cause of death is attributed to such diseases as smallpox, diphtheria, or the plague and embalming is done out of public health concerns). I kept thinking about that not-so-distant era when doctors were routinely cutting babies out of anaesthetized mothers, closing the door on a father left to worry and wait out of sight in another room under the notion that this operation was somehow better than proceeding naturally.

What I did come away with is, perhaps, a better understanding of why I encountered so many closed doors. I believe ultimately it has less to do with privacy than the fact that if more people got a glimpse of what happens to their loved ones after they've taken their last breath, there'd be a hell of a rush on pine boxes, scented bath oils and incense.

The Eleventh Week

 Wherein a state adopts legal amendments that rob families of rights and money by allowing the funeral industry to hold a loved one's body for ransom.

Every state has its share of strange and downright stupid laws. If you are from Michigan, you may remember the free speech case involving a Roseville man who violated an 1897 state statute against the use of "indecent, immoral, obscene, vulgar or insulting language in the presence or hearing of any woman or child." After hitting a rock and tipping his canoe on the Rifle River, Timothy Boomer, 25, cussed up a blue streak so riddled with f-bombs (50 to 75 in several minutes, according to witness reports) that he not only landed in a Standish court with ACLU legal counsel, but also on the front page of newspapers from the *Seattle Post-Intelligencer* to the *Chicago Sun-Times*. More recently, in December 2008, Brighton, Michigan city officials put a ban on public displays of "annoying behavior." Imagine this coming from a state that spawned the likes of Michael Moore (a bone for my right-leaning readers) *and* Ted Nugent (ditto for the left)—a state where Unibomber Ted Kaczinski and uber-bitch Ann Coulter went to college.

We have laws on the books that say adultery is a felony punishable by life in prison. Intruders have the right to sue you if they are injured while burglarizing your home. Throwing an octopus on the ice at the Joe Louis Arena during a Red Wings' game can get you tossed in the clink (apparently, this is a problem). A twelve-year-old can legally own a handgun, but motorists who dangle objects like fuzzy dice and garter belts from their rearview mirrors are considered such a hazard to themselves and others that doing so can get you pulled over and possibly thrown in the clink. (This just happened back in January to a man named Lonnie Ray Davis. Davis never denied that he was packing a loaded handgun, cocaine, an open pint of Hennessey cognac, and an invalid driver's license in his car when pulled over late one night by Westland-area police. But lawyers for Davis challenged Michigan's "dangling objects law" as unconstitutional after troopers admitted with a straight face that a Tweety Bird air freshener hanging from Davis' mirror was their only justification for the stop.)

Yes, you can homeschool your children, you can have a home birth, you can send an aging parent to a nursing home or, if you choose, take care of them yourself.

"You don't have to hire an accountant to do your taxes. And even if you're sick and dying you can still refuse to go to a hospital," adds Wendy Lyons, a Detroit-area home funeral advocate and president of the 2,000 member Funeral Consumers Information Society. "So why does Michigan mandate that families must hire a funeral director? I consider it a basic civil right: Who gets to decide who our dead belong to?"

I'd called Lyons to find out what kind of paperwork a person planning a home funeral might need to pull together, but ended up getting a crash course on why families (and the dying) in the good state of Michigan lose all their rights the moment a loved one takes their last breath.

In Louisiana, Virginia, and Oklahoma only a funeral director is allowed to sell caskets. In New York, Connecticut, Nebraska and Indiana you are legally bound to hire an undertaker. But in 2003, the Michigan legislature began setting the state dismally apart when it decreed that funeral director "certification" is required on every death certificate. A 2006 law further required *any* handling of a body be under the supervision of a funeral director.

"Funeral law in the state was always sort of vague and never friendly to families, but these amendments sort of cinched it," says Lyons. Until recently, Utah was the only other state in the nation that had similar restrictions (a law requiring citizens to hire a funeral director that also, coincidently, sailed through the legislature that same year). After three years and a lot of work, outraged citizens led by the Funeral Consumers Alliance were successful in restoring their rights in Utah. Now, in Lyons' opinion, that leaves Michigan standing alone as the worst state in the nation when talking about funeral law and the rights of citizens to care for their own dead.

Prior to 2006, Michigan funeral law allowed for a funeral director "or person acting as a funeral director" to assume custody of a dead body and "obtain authorization for the final disposition." The law at the time *did not* say that only a funeral director must report the death—or, for that matter, assume first and chief authority over the body. But no more, according to Lyons.

Now, when you or a family member dies, you have to open your door and your wallet to a funeral director whether you want to or not. Die unprepared in a Michigan hospital and the person at your bedside—wife, husband, mother, brother, best friend—has absolutely no legal right to take your body anywhere let alone take charge in seeing that your last requests are carried out.

In the cases of non-traditional unions, Michigan is even more rigid and unfriendly with funeral law saying that next of kin—and only legal next of kin—can make arrangements for the deceased. A brother you haven't talked to or seen in a couple decades or a father who went to the store late one night for diapers and formula and never came back—they trump the funeral and burial wishes of a best friend or same-sex life partner.

How did this happen?

Was it public apathy? The power of the Michigan Funeral Directors Association?

When asked what, in her opinion, opened the door to the new laws, Lyons prefaced her words—"Well, the legislature doesn't come up with these ideas on their own"—by saying that she believed funeral directors performed a valuable service to people who wanted it.

But, according to Lyons, the roughly 1,300-member Michigan Funeral Directors Association —founded in 1860 and the oldest group of its kind in the United States—wields tremendous lobbying power with state politicians whose constituents don't seem to know or care about the issue.

Wondering how much influence the MFDA really had, I dug up an article in the *Detroit Metro Times* (January 2009) that said MFDA members paid more than $530,000 in dues and assessments in 2007. "The Michigan Campaign Finance Network ranked the state association's political action committee—lobby arm—as 95th in spending in the state's top 150 during the 2008 election cycle as of the end of October." My copy of the Michigan Campaign Finance Network's "Top 200" lobbyists ranked the MFDA 85th. Either way, the organization spent so much money on lobbying that they ranked higher on the list than the United Auto Workers, Johnson & Johnson, Philip Morris and Anheuser-Busch.

Michigan has had on average about 86,000 deaths each year since 2000. It doesn't take an expert to see that the new state laws go a long way to helping beef up the bottom line of a national industry. Figures from the National Funeral Directors Association say nearly 22,000 funeral homes generate $11 billion annually.

According to figures from the Funeral Consumers Alliance, families who do not wish to involve a funeral director in the death and burial of a loved one must now pay as much as $1,200 to one anyway. Lyons believed that estimate a little high, telling me she has found funeral directors who will charge as little as $800 for "certifying" the death certificate and "supervising" a direct cremation.

I had to wonder out loud, though: if the state requires you to hire a funeral director even if you don't want to, shouldn't the state be the one paying the bill?

Lyons has heard many people in the green burial and home funeral movement asking the same question.

In the 44 other states that permit family-directed funerals without the involvement of a funeral director, I learned that pulling the paperwork together for the purpose of planning your own green burial and home funeral was relatively simple. Some states, like Vermont, actually support families by offering information online to those wanting to take charge of their own dead. Nora Cedarwind Young, the death midwife who gave me the over-the-phone primer on the intricacies of the profession, had a list she called the "six essential documents" everyone should have in relation to death. (A state-specific list is also available online).

- *Will*
- *Health Care Directive/Living Will*

- *Durable Power of Attorney Health*
- *Durable Power of Attorney Finance*
- *Disposition of Body Form*
- *HIPPA (authorization forms, patient consent, privacy practices)*

Young directed me to her website for a copy of the list and recommended I look it over and regularly update these documents every year—"Pick a date. Open a bottle of wine," she told me. "Then, put the file in a safety deposit box and tell everyone close to you that it's there."

Back on the phone with Wendy Lyons, I asked her, "Here in Michigan where the rules are different, what is a person to do?"

My wife and I had already set up a will. The HIPPA forms were easy enough to find online. But while it's still legal for Michiganders to care for their dead, the fact is you can't simply call the local county clerk or registrar to get a death certificate, disposition permit or, for that matter, any of the necessary paperwork to make for a legal burial or cremation (the latter of which also required the signature of the local coroner before you could proceed). All very confusing. Lyons agreed:

"The Michigan laws compound the confusion and fear people already have about death and burial, and that the loved one is not only taken away spiritually but physically by strangers."

Lyons repeated that she didn't believe that funeral directors, as a group, were bad. Most were caring people not out to take advantage of consumers. But there were certainly a few in positions of influence, she said, who consider themselves "gatekeepers" of funeral rites and services.

Lyons did a good a job of not coming across as angry or cynical, but that didn't make Michigan's burial law any easier for me to swallow. The fact is that now only people like Lyons, who have spent a considerable portion of their life planning the details of their death and burial, have any real shot at avoiding the added expense and unwanted violation of privacy that comes with having to hire a funeral director.

I didn't need Lyons to tell me that the current system puts the consumer at a troubling disadvantage. Unlike a wedding or a birth, a typical funeral is hastily planned in about two or three days. At what is presumably one of the most emotionally taxing points in a person's life—a point when the consumer is made to believe they are pressed for time and certainly not in the right frame of mind to be an intelligent or discerning shopper—a funeral director has the legal ability to inhibit or facilitate the burial of a loved one for prices rarely if ever challenged by the bereaved.

"Michigan burial law is interpreted by the funeral industry to mean that [after death] an unembalmed body must be cremated or buried within forty-eight hours," said Lyons.

But it turns out the "48 Hour Rule" in Michigan is a myth. In fact, aside from cases where death was caused by rabidly infectious diseases such as smallpox and bubonic plague, embalming is rarely required by law. Lyons later sent me a copy of the Funeral Consumers Information Society newsletter, *Egress*, that contained an article by Michigan Mortuary Science Licensee Erika Nelson, who traced the erroneous belief back to an out-dated Michigan funeral statue (R325-1141).

"This rule was created in a time when the shipment of biological materials was considered unsafe due to the inability to properly refrigerate or contain them," wrote Nelson, adding that this law only pertains to cases where a body "leaves the hands of one funeral director, is moved by train, plane, boat or other 'common carrier' and reaches the hands of another funeral director In a different jurisdiction."

Lyons and Nelson agreed most funeral directors interpret this law to mean that embalming is required for all bodies in order to allow for transportation to a cemetery or crematory for disposition.

"Funeral directors are afraid that they will be breaking the rule if they do not insist that this happen," continued Nelson. "The truth of the matter is that the rule would generally not apply to local transport, and there is no enforceable punishment for disregarding the rule."

As president of the Funeral Consumers Information Society, Lyons told me she would like to see some clarification of the "48 Hour Rule," specifically a change that allows for refrigeration or dry ice cooling as an alternative to embalming. Lyons believes the current reading of the law makes it very difficult for families to avoid a loved one having to go through the ghastly invasive and toxic embalming procedure. It also puts unnecessary pressure and an added financial burden on families who, for instance, might want a traditional home wake that could last anywhere from two to four days. Lyons is also working toward a repeal of the 2003 and 2006 amendments that respectively mandate that the handling and disposition of a body "shall be under the supervision of a person licensed to practice mortuary science in this state" and that death certificates be signed by a licensed funeral director. She would also like to see a law created that protects the right of families and "faith communities" to care for their dead without a funeral director.

Maybe someday Lyons will get her wish. Until then, her advice to me was to get busy trying to find a green-leaning funeral director.

The Twelfth Week

 **Wherein a search for meaning ends in a place where there is none.**

Three months ago I never intended to visit my father's grave. Was it 15 or 20 years since the last time I'd been there? I could never get it clear. I couldn't even remember the name of the cemetery, it had been so long. Over the years, anytime I had thought about the place, the only thing I could recall was that there was an evergreen tree—a great big hemlock I think—near his bronze marker on the hill. I also remembered a World War II artillery cannon and, instead of flowers, an entire field of tiny, flapping American flags blossoming out of the turf. All this time and 700 miles away in Michigan, what I most recalled from my last visit to the cemetery was the drive to Annville, Pennsylvania—a gray blur of grimy strip malls, stoplights, traffic and sagging electrical wires lining Route 422. Sprawling sameness, the occasional smoke stack and telephone poles instead of trees. Now, on a foggy day late in December, with my mother behind the wheel, it seemed like the place had only gotten drearier. The ex-WWF wrestler Steve Blackman was born in Annville, a suburb of a suburb of a suburb. I guess you could say its dreariness could drive one into a job that requires one be comfortable with getting periodically kicked in the head.

In New York, it's estimated that as many as 60,000 of the city residents who die every year are exported to cemeteries outside the city limits. Graveyards in the city are just too full. And not only in New York. I read similar stories coming out of Chicago, Salt Lake and a smattering of major cities in between.

Cemeteries on military bases, like Fort Riley in Kansas and Fort Snelling in Minnesota, are even worse off. They've been stacking them in Arlington National Cemetery since 1962, when Congress first passed the law allowing family to be buried in the same grave with fallen service members. According to an August 2008 report of the *Arlington Connection*, more than 300,000 people are already buried there with an average increase of 6,500 each year. The 624-acre cemetery along the Potomac River is expected to be fully occupied by 2030.

London cemeteries are also running out of space. The problem is so dire that, according to the report in *The London Times* online, authorities across that country were expected to begin exhuming remains and reburying them deeper "to make more room on top."

Over the past twelve weeks, I'd developed something of an eye for cemeteries. Or maybe I should say I became more aware of them. In my mind, scenically speaking, cemeteries were a lot like golf courses. Both amounted to tracts of predominantly treeless, overly-landscaped parcels of land that hold no redeeming value to anyone who doesn't have a vested interest in the property—either by connection to a deceased family member or an ability to swing a five iron.

I understand people could say the same thing about the spaces I hold dear—swamps and fields and woodlots choked with briars and brambles and rabbit brush. I understand that I'm the oddball here.

Still, I wonder. An average 18-hole, 72-par golf course requires anywhere from 140 to 180 acres of land. A 9-hole course is roughly half that. No such figures seem to exist for the average-sized cemetery in America. How much land in this country is already set aside for conventional cemeteries? No one could tell me.

Every time I'm back east in "BosWash"—a term coined by French geographer Jean Gottmman in his book *Megalopolis: The Urbanized Northeast Seaboard of the United States*—I can't help but think this place could use any excuse for open space—at least some trees, for God's sake—that it could get.

A popular argument from those in favor of more back-to-nature green burial preserves is that as a desirable by-product, preserves actually save land. In many American cities, cemeteries are the only open space left. But, taking emotion out of it for a second, isn't a cemetery really just a dumping ground? You can't toss a football in an urban graveyard without bouncing it off a headstone and, more likely, getting yourself arrested. There are no shady trees to have picnics under. No scenic trails for walking.

I want to say Grandview Memorial Park—my father's cemetery on the outskirts of town—was nicer than a lot of cemeteries I'd seen. But really, aside from a couple big evergreens, it was pretty much the same as any other. In the fog, we nearly missed the turn off Route 422. My mother saw it first and, without a word, jacked the steering wheel left, cutting across traffic with me gripping the dash. We drove over the railroad tracks, up the hill and through the gate. Once around the grounds we cruised, unsure if my father was buried at the top of the hill or more in the middle.

We rolled past one other car parked in the foggy gloom. Inside a rather rotund woman sat in the driver's seat clutching a mobile phone to her ear with one hand and making hacking gestures over the steering wheel with the other. The week after Christmas, many of the graves were marked with bunches of flowers and wreaths tied with red bows. A few had actual Christmas trees, little Charlie Brown evergreens in cheap plastic pots, festively adorned with ornaments, tinsel and ribbon.

My father's grave was just another of the hundreds of bronze markers on the ground. I found it first and called my mother over.

"Oh, look," she said. "Yeah, there it is!"

Upon seeing it after all these years, I hoped I'd feel something profound. But I didn't. There was not even any real moment of silence, although the way my father died and was buried is exactly the reason I decided that, if I had anything to say about it, there was no way I was going out the same way. Now I was here, standing over his grave, trying to eke out some sort of meaning—a little affirmation would have been nice, some sort of sign that this path I took up twelve weeks was the right one.

My mother spoke first:

"You know, Bob, your father's not there anymore. This here is just a memorial."

And she was right.

I couldn't have felt more distant from the memory of my father than at that moment. There were no warm memories or forgotten recollections of moments we spent together while he was alive. Instead I recalled nothing but the day of his funeral, particularly walking up to his coffin as a boy and thinking, more or less, *Who the hell is that?* I remembered that someone, maybe my grandmother, whispered that it was okay to touch it, that it was time to say goodbye to that alien, almost unrecognizable corpse. When I cried on that day, it wasn't even for the loss of him. It was because when I looked around at everyone else it seemed at that scheduled time, that hour or so, the thing you were supposed to do. And with that I had this overwhelming feeling that coming here was wrong. Standing over that marker there was only a palatable feeling of boyish helplessness and sadness . . . and not because he was gone. In fact, the father I chose to remember was everywhere *but* here. And I couldn't turn away from that strange place fast enough, to get away from there and get back to more familiar ground.

Is twelve weeks really enough time to plan a green burial?

On the way home, my mother wanted to know. After "what is a green burial," this is the question I was most often asked and, three months later, I would have to say both "yes" and "no."

I think you can get all the paperwork together, put your wish list neatly in a file and carefully update it every year. But as for pulling off the burial itself, I'm convinced that takes a lifetime of diligent planning and re-planning—not to mention friends and family as determined as you are to see those wishes carried out.

After twelve weeks, I was still looking for a green-leaning funeral director willing to sign off on a home funeral. Of course, even if I manage to find and befriend one, my hope is not to die for many years. What's to say my funeral director will even be around to rescue me from the hospital crows? I had work yet to do constructing my coffin. And since you're not going anywhere in a pine box without the support of friends and family, there was always this question of who would actually be there to put my last wishes into play. What's to say the friends I ask to spirit my body out into the woods and dig my grave will even be around ten, twenty, thirty years from now?

On the way home, I told my mother a little bit about my burial plan and then she told me hers.

"Being buried under the ground," she gripped the wheel and shivered. "That's always gristled me."

Truly, I never had my mom pegged as a traditional cremation kind of gal, but that was her plan. No viewing for her. No embalming. Looking at my mother behind the wheel of the car, I thought how little she'd changed over the years. She's still sitting upright at the wheel, staring dead ahead, never without a plan. Not wishing to be a burden on anybody, she told me that she already had everything drawn up.

"Everything's taken care of," she said.

I could heap on the adjectives to describe my mother, but those four words pretty much sum the woman up. The embodiment of hard-edged stoicism, my mother's the kind of woman who, after divorcing my father years before anybody knew there was a tumor in his head, never spoke a bad word in front of me about the man.

The stop-and-go drive home from Annville was a long one, so there was ample time to talk about that, too, and my mother said things about my father that she never told me before. She answered questions that, without the subject of green burial to break new ground between us, had never before felt appropriate to ask. It was as if some new and deeper kind of trusting space had opened between us. Throughout the last twelve weeks, the subject of green burial made me more conscious of how I listened to people.

For three months, I thought about death more intensely than I think the average person should have to. But in an odd sort of way that was also the best part, too—that maybe in trying to die and be buried green I may now live my life a little bit better, too.

Lake Ann, January 2009

Suggested Reading

Creating Home Funerals
www.finalpassages.org
A comprehensive three-booklet set detailing everything from legal planning to the preparation of the deceased for a home funeral and viewing.

Undertaken With Love: A Home Funeral Guide for Congregations and Communities
www.homefuneralmanual.org
A 40-page guide for church and social groups that instructs on how to start a home funeral committee; how to research and identify your legal rights; how to handle, bathe and transport the body; and how to sustain an effective home funeral committee.

Caring for the Dead: Your Final Act of Love
by Lisa Carlson
A comprehensive tome on funeral law for the consumer. The laws and regulations of each state are described in easy-to-understand language, with listings of "consumer concerns" in states that have inadequate protections for consumers. The individual chapters for each state also include contact information for medical schools that have a need for body donations, crematories and local non-profit memorial societies, as well as specific statewide cautions about dealing with funeral and cemetery establishments.

Before I Go, You Should Know—Funeral Planning Kit
www.funerals.org
An end-of-life planning kit from the Funeral Consumers Alliance that comes in a plastic button-tie pouch with a state-specific living will and other advance medical directives, plus a 16-page write-in booklet with illustrations by Edward Gorey.

Dealing Creatively with Death: A Manual of Death Education and Simple Burial
by Ernest Morgan
A small encyclopedia on death-related problems (social, emotional, philosophical and practical), this classic volume also focuses on ways to simplify funeral arrangements, cremation and body and organ donation.

*Grave Matters: A Journey Through the Modern Funeral
Industry to a Natural Way of Burial*
by Mark Harris
Grave Matters follows families who found in "green" burial a more
natural, more economic, and ultimately more meaningful alternative
to the tired and toxic send-off on offer at the local funeral parlor. The
book details the embalming process and the environmental aftermath of
the standard funeral. Harris also traces the history of burial in America,
from frontier cemeteries to the billion-dollar business it is today,
reporting on real families who opted for more simple, natural returns.

I Died Laughing: Funeral Education with a Light Touch
by Lisa Carlson
The author, a long-time consumer advocate, has regaled her audience
for years with funeral humor as an ice-breaker for discussion of
consumer issues in dealing with the funeral industry. This book is
full of her favorite jokes and witticisms, each chapter ending with a
few pages called "But Seriously . . ." containing selected information
to help you become a more educated consumer. Illustrations by the
immortal Edward Gorey.

The American Way of Death Revisited
by Jessica Mitford
A scathing yet witty critique of the funeral industry. In this classic,
Mitford uses the industry's own words to make her points.

You Only Die Once: Preparing for the End of Life with Grace and Gusto
by Margie Jenkins
A stimulating and compelling case that preparing for life's ending is
the groundwork for living a more bodacious and rewarding life. Using
stories and personal experiences, the book highlights the benefits and
importance of being informed about end-of-life decisions that you can
make now.

Suggested Viewing

A Family Undertaking
A PBS documentary by Elizabeth Westrate that explores the growing home-funeral movement. Follows several families in their most intimate moments as they reclaim the end of life, forgoing a typical mortuary funeral to care for their loved ones at home. Available through Netflix.

Passing Through Our Hands
www.passingthroughourhands.com
A step-by-step instructional video on how to provide after-death care of the body.

Green Burial Advocacy and Resources

Crossings: Caring For Our Own At Death
7108 Holly Avenue, Takoma Park, MD 20912
www.crossings.net
Crossings is a non-profit home funeral and green burial resource center providing information designed to help those who wish to bring after-death care back into family and community life.

Green Burial Council
550 D, St. Michaels Drive, Santa Fe, NM 87508
888.966.3330
www.greenburialcouncil.org
An independent, non-profit organization founded to encourage ethical and sustainable practices in the death care industry. The Council has established "green certified" protocols for cemetery site selection, memorial nature preserve operators, funeral providers and cremation facilities.

The Natural Burial Co-operative, Inc.
14 Division Street, Guelph, ON, N1H 1P9, Canada
www.naturalburial.ca
The Natural Burial C0-operative is an on-line Canadian resource and information center that promotes natural burial funeral services and products that enhance, protect and preserve the natural environment.

Memorial Ecosystems
www.memorialecosystems.com
Formed in 1996 by Dr. Billy Campbell, Memorial Ecosystems offers
consulting services in conservation burial set-up and start-up,
creating partnerships and joint ventures.

Funeral Consumers Alliance
33 Patchen Road, South Burlington, VT 05403
800.765.0107
www.funerals.org
Funeral Consumers Alliance is a nonprofit organization dedicated to
protecting a consumer's right to choose a meaningful, dignified,
affordable funeral. The FCA offers pamphlets and newsletters on
choices to increase public awareness of funeral options, including how
to care for your own dead without using a funeral home. The FCA also
monitors funeral industry trends and practices nationally and exposes
abuses while serving as a consumer advocate for legal and regulatory
reform, giving advice on or lobbying for necessary changes.

Funeral Consumers Information Society
PO Box 24054, Detroit, MI 48224
www.funeralinformationsociety.org
Established in 1961, the volunteer-led Funeral Consumers
Information Society was founded to promote preplanning for simple,
dignified final rites. Today, the Society's role has expanded to reflect a
growing need for information about other related issues. Through its
information and referral services, speakers' bureau, newsletters and
educational literature, FCIS offers up-to-date information on federal
and state legislation, current literature and practical considerations
for informed planning.

Trust for Natural Legacies, Inc.
222 S. Hamilton Street, Suite #1, Madison, WI 53703
www.naturallegacies.org
A non-profit land trust that preserves and restores natural areas by
owning, operating and promoting nature preserves throughout the
Midwest. One of TNL's goals is to see natural burial preserves opened
in every state in the region.

Funeral Ethics Organization
PO Box 145, Hinesburg, VT 05461
802.482.3437
www.funeralethics.org
FEO's mission is to promote ethical dealings in all death-related transactions by working for better understanding of ethical issues among funeral, cemetery, memorial industry practitioners, law enforcement, organ procurement organizations and state agencies, as well as better understanding between these and the general public.

Earth-Friendly Caskets and Coffins

Natural Burial Company
PO Box 11204, Eugene, Oregon 97440
www.naturalburialcompany.com
The largest supplier of eco-friendly caskets, cremation urns and environmentally friendly burial products in America. The Natural Burial Company offers retail-direct options for families who are managing their own funeral.

ARK Wood Caskets
www.arkwoodcaskets.com
No nails, stains, varnish, or metal—ARK wood coffins are shipped and store flat and can be assembled in about half an hour.

Boot Hill Coffins
www.boothillcoffins.net
Earth-friendly, Old West style coffins "tested up to 400 pounds" and built to "accommodate western-style boots and hats."

Last Things
www.lastthings.net
Unique yet simple, handmade wood coffins. The website also offers free plans for constructing a simple pine box-style coffin.

Casket Furniture
www.casketfurniture.com
Casket plans, kits and novelties. Specializing in caskets that double as bookshelves, coffee tables, pool tables, couches and entertainment centers.

Ecoffins USA
www.ecoffinsusa.com
Makers of hand-woven bamboo and banana sheaf caskets with an
"eco-ply board." Base-engineered to accommodate up to 325 pounds.

Griffith Woodworks
www.griffithwoodworks.com
Exquisitely crafted pine coffins made one at a time by a master
woodworking craftsman.

Cremation Products, Inc.
www.cremationproductsinc.com
Air transport coffin containers and bio-degradable cardboard coffins
suitable for green burial and cremation.

Colorful Coffins
www.colorfulcoffins.com
Providers of biodegradable cremation urns and coffins made from
bamboo, pandanus, banana sheaf and willow. Simple pine boxes and
basket-style coffins and unique hand-painted cremation gourds.
Specializing in uniquely designed cardboard and wood coffins that
can be personalized with a decorative theme prior to shipping or by
the consumer at home.

Kent Casket
www.kentcasket.com
Solid pine caskets—either standard box or toe pincher-style—
advertised as suitable for burial or cremation. Totally biodegradable
and made without toxic varnishes or glue. Shipped flat and assemble
in minutes.

Green Casket Company
www.greencasket.net
Casket and casket-kits constructed from solid pine grown from
sustainable North Carolina forests. A family-owned company.

No Name Lumber
www.nonamelumber.com
Makers of recycled wood coffins made from recycled shipping pallets
and scrape lumber. No assembly required.

Burials Shrouds

Kinkaraco
www.kinkaraco.com
Makers of biodegradable, American-made burial shrouds, cremation shrouds, removal shrouds and other ceremonial funeral products for the consumer, funeral homes and cemeteries all over the USA and around the world.

Janazah Kits
Modest Garb c/o Al-Furqan Bookstore and Bazaar
1104 E. Vernon Road, Philadelphia, PA 19150
www.modestgarb.com
Providers of Janazah kits that include everything needed for the burial of the deceased according to Islamic custom. The Complete Shroud Kit ($65) comes with bath sponge, wash cloth, bar soap, hair shampoo, camphor oil, tie cloths, three pairs of gloves and a book on death preparation and prayers. Made in USA.

White Eagle Memorial Preserve
401 Ekone Road, Goldendale, WA 98620
www.naturalburialground.com
Makers of handmade, natural and biodegradeable burial shrouds.

Natural Burial Preserves in America

The number of natural burial preserves in America has been growing steadily every year. This combined with the rising number of conventional cemeteries that are starting to set aside land for clients who desire natural burial means that this list is in no way comprehensive. For the most up-to-date listing near you, go to the website for Green Burial Council (www.greenburialcouncil.org) or The Centre for Natural Burial (www.naturalburial.coop).

Cedar Brook Burial Ground
175 Boothby Road, Limington, ME 04049
207.637.2085
www.greencemetery.blogspot.com

Eternal Rest Memories Park
2966 Belcher Road, Dunedin, FL 34698
727.733.2300
www.eternalrest.com

Ethician Family Cemetery
1401 19th Street, Huntsville, TX 77340
936.581.4302
www.ethicianfamilycemetery.org

Forever Fernwood
301 Tennessee Valley Road, Mill Valley, CA 94941
415.383.7100
www.foreverfernwood.com

Foxfield Preserve Nature Cemetery
PO Box 202, Wilmot, OH 44689
330.763.1331
www.foxfieldpreserve.org

Glendale Memorial Nature Preserve
97 Railroad Avenue, DeFuniak Springs, FL 32433
850.859.2141
www.glendalenaturepreserve.org

Greensprings Natural Cemetery
293 Irish Hill Road, Newfield, NY 14867
607.564.7577
www.naturalburial.org

Honey Creek Woodlands
212 Highway 212 S.W. , Conyers, GA 30094
770.483.7535
www.honeycreekwoodlands.com

Lakeview Memorial Cemetery & Mortuary
1640 East Lakeview Drive, Bountiful, UT 84010
801.298.1564

Ramsey Creek Preserve
111 W. Main Street, Westminster, SC 29693
864.647.7798
www.ramseycreekpreserve.com

Commonwealth Conservancy
117 N. Guadalupe Street, Suite C, Santa Fe, NM 87501
505.982.0071
www.commonwealconservancy.org

The Union Cemetery
5442 Somers Point Road, Rt. 559, Mays Landing, NJ 08330
609.625.7571
www.theunioncemetery.com

White Eagle Memorial Preserve
401 Ekone Road, Goldendale, WA 98620
206.350.7353
www.naturalburialground.com

Home Funerals

This Home Funeral Guide Directory was compiled by Crossings: Caring for Our Own, a national educational organization dedicated to the renewal of home funeral and traditional green burial care. More information at www.crossings.net.

CALIFORNIA
A Family Farewell and Colorful Coffins
Jane Hillhouse
Palo Alto
jane@solution1.biz

Final Passages
Jerrigrace Lyons
PO Box 1721, Sebastopol, CA 95473
707.824.0268
www.finalpassages.org / info@finalpassages.org

Nancy Poer
5595 White Feather Way, Placerville, CA 95667
530.622.9302
www.nancyjewelpoer.com / nancypoer@directcon.net

Heidi Boucher
heidiboucher@aol.com (referred by Nancy Poer at her website)

Thresholds
Barbara Kernan
8719 Los Coches Road, Lakeside, CA 92040
619.390.1411
www.thresholds.us / homefunerals@cox.net

COLORADO
Natural Transitions Funeral Guidance
Karen van Vuuren
PO Box 17848, Boulder, CO 80308
303.443.3418
www.naturaltransitions.org
info@naturaltransitions.org / Karen@totalspeed.net

MARYLAND
Crossings: Caring for Our Own at Death
Beth Knox
7108 Holly Avenue, Takoma Park, MD 20912
301.523.3033
www.crossings.net / crossingcare@earthlink.net

IDAHO
Susan Randall and Mary Jane Oresik
Ida Home Funerals, LLC

MAINE
Richard Ailes
PO Box 997, Camden, ME 04843
Richardailes@aol.com

MICHIGAN
Wendy Lyons
Detroit FCA board (Beth's and Jerrigrace's workshops)
lyonslair@comcast.net

Erika Nelson, FN, SW
erika.beth.nelson@gmail.com
401 W. Geneva Drive, Dewitt, MI 48820
517.285.3630

Maria Lyzen
Rochester (Beth's workshop)
mlyzen@msn.com

Helaine Hunscher
Ann Arbor FCA (Beth's workshop)
hunscher@umich.edu

Tammy Corwin-Renner
Ann Arbor (Threshold Choir director)

MINNESOTA
Jean Madsen and Michael Sorrell Portages
Created to support families in creating vigils and family directed
funerals in the Twin Cities area. Guidebooks available.
portagesafa@yahoo.com

Ellen Hofschmidt
Ritualist, sacred body washing. Teaches courses.
Twin Cities area

Threshold Group: Conscious Living...Conscious Dying
Linda Bergh
612.927.0894
www.linda@lindabergh.org

Marianne Dietzel
651.633.0432
m_dietzel@yahoo.com

NEW MEXICO
Juliet Armstrong (and Joe Sehee)
Santa Fe

Green Burial Council
505.603.9301

NEW YORK
Jonatha Haase
10 Green River Lane, Hillsdale, NY 12529
518.325.7454

Christian Community connection
Ann-Elizabeth Barnes and Richard Meyer
Harlemville (event with Nancy Poer)

NORTH CAROLINA
Kathleen Zimmer, FN
Charlottesville (Beth's workshop)
Hill and Wood Funeral Home

Sandy LaGrega
Greensboro
336.292.7947
SunSan52@aol.com

OHIO
Ann S.
Hospice volunteer coordinator
ha7901@aol.com

TEXAS
Donna Belk
512.922.8043

Sandy Booth
512.440.7979

Leslie Pearson
512.264.2137
www.crossingscircle.org
donnabelk@gmail.com, sdbooth@sbcglobal.net,
wapiticlan@yahoo.com

Susan Oppie
402 Mission Street #4, San Antonio, TX 78210
210.241.2889
vivamemorialartr@hotmail.com

VERMONT
Patty Dunn
hospice volunteer services
Middlebury
802.388.4111

WASHINGTON
Char Barrett, FN
Hospice volunteer, celebrant (trained with Jerrigrace Lyons)
1801 12th Avenue, Suite A, Seattle, WA 98122
206.529.3803
www.asacredmoment.com / char_barrett@yahoo.com

DeAnna Elliott, RN, CHPN
Hospice experience (trained with Jerrigrace)
DeeCElliott@comcast.net

Annie McManus
baseballmonkeye@eathlink.net

Nora Cedarwind Young
PO Box 187, Chimacum, WA 98325
360.732.0126

Ceremonies for Life's Thresholds
www.thresholdsoflife.org / cedarwind@tscnet.com

Anna And David Copley
253.854.7021
Anna@TheFuneralSite.com
TheFuneralSite.com / TheGreenFuneralSite.com

WISCONSIN
Lucy Basler
Retired hospice chaplain
lucybasler@gmail.com

Kathy Gardipee
Calumetville and Fond du Lac)

Funeral Alternatives

Charlene Elderkin
Threshold Circle, Viroqua
elderkin@mwt.net

The Invisible Community
Robert Lord
Robert@theinvisiblecommunity.org
www.theinvisiblecommunity.org

Death Midwifery Classes and Seminars

Final Passages
PO Box 1721, Sebastopol, CA 95473
707.824.0268
www.finalpassages.org
Final Passages founder Jerrigrace Lyons is a nationally known leader in the home funeral movement who regularly offers training, seminars and workshops on the art of death midwifery.

Crossings
7108 Holly Avenue, Takoma Park, MD 20912
www.crossings.net
Crossing offers hands-on workshops on the principles, practice and procedures for naturally caring for the dead. Direct educational support services are available in the Washington, DC, metropolitan area and throughout the country. Consult website for rates and a full description of services provided.

Nora Cedarwind Young
www.thresholdsoflife.org
Certified death midwife Nora Cedarwind Young is based in
Washington state but regularly conducts green burial and death
midwifery workshops at gatherings and conferences throughout
the Pacific Northwest and across the nation.

Rebekah S. Benner
www.ahomefuneral.com

Death midwife and certified grief recovery specialist, Rebekah Benner
is based in Ohio. She offers home funeral assistance and green burial
consulting services.

Finding a Death Midwife

Funeral Consumers Alliance
33 Patchen Road, South Burlington, VT 05403
800.765.0107
www.funerals.org
The Funeral Consumers Alliance website makes available, free of
charge, a state-by-state affiliate's directory. FCA affiliates are
volunteer-run, nonsectarian and provide a local source of funeral
planning information, including how to find a death midwife or
"green-leaning" funeral directory near you. Click on "Find
A Local FCA."

About the Author

Bob Butz is an award winning book author, essayist, past contributing editor to *Sports Afield* and freelance magazine writer whose by-line has appeared in the *New York Times*, *GQ*, *Land Rover Journal*, *National Wildlife*, *Outdoor Life*, *Men's Journal* and *Field and Stream*. In 2006, Butz's book *Beast of Never, Cat of God: The Search for the Eastern Puma* received a Michigan Notable Book Award from the Library of Michigan. He is also the author of *An Uncrowded Place* released by Huron River Press in 2008. Butz lives in northern Michigan with his wife, Nancy, and their two children. For more information, check out www.bobbutz.com.